Children's Reading

This book is the result of a major national survey which aimed to discover the books children choose to read and why. This topic regularly raises high levels of anxiety and moralism as adults witness changes in children's reading habits and worry about the sensationalism and consumerism which might influence their children.

The *Children's Reading Choices* project replicates a seminal study published in 1977, and allows a picture to be drawn of changes in children's voluntary reading over a quarter of a century. These changes are fully documented and discussed, and the book investigates such topics as: children's favourite authors and series; the gendered nature of children's reading; quality in children's literature; comic, magazine and newspaper reading; the influence of family reading habits; the relationship between reading, computers and television; the reading experiences of children for whom English is an additional language; children's library use.

If we are to prepare children for the literacy demands of the future we need hard information and wide-ranging debate. We need to know what children do read rather than what we wish they would read. This study provides a snapshot of children's reading at a particular moment, as well as identifying trends in children's reading over a period of two decades. *Children's Reading Choices* provides an invaluable resource for teachers, librarians, parents, publishers and all those concerned to understand the changing nature of children's reading habits.

Dr Christine Hall and **Dr Martin Coles** both teach at the University of Nottingham.

Children's Reading Choices

Christine Hall and
Martin Coles

London and New York

First published 1999
by Routledge
11 New Fetter Lane, London EC4P 4EE

Simultaneously published in the USA and Canada
by Routledge
29 West 35th Street, New York, NY 10001

Typeset in Palatino by Keystroke, Jacaranda Lodge, Wolverhampton
Printed and bound in Great Britain by Clays Ltd, St Ives PLC

British Library Cataloguing in Publication Data
A catalogue record for this book is available from the British Library

Library of Congress Cataloging in Publication Data
Coles, Martin, 1952–
    Children's reading choices / Christine Hall and Martin Coles.
      p.   cm.
      1. Children—Great Britain—Books and reading. I. Hall,
Christine. II. Title.
Z1037.A1C56 1999
028.5'0941—dc21   98–36491
                                              CIP

ISBN 0–415–18387–1

For Alice and Tom, Rebecca and Charlotte

Contents

Tables

Introduction

This is a book about what children *choose* to read. This is a topic which is of concern to several different groups of people: parents and teachers (frequently), politicians and the media (intermittently) and, of course, children themselves. It is a topic which can raise high levels of anxiety and moralism as adults contemplate perceived changes in reading habits and worry about sensationalism, consumerism and all the other possibly malign 'isms' which might influence their children.

In this book we discuss, amongst other issues, changing literacy patterns, adult anxieties and judgements about quality. Our discussions are rooted in information gathered from nearly 8,000 10, 12- and 14-year-old children across England. We have followed up the survey by holding discussions with a large number of children, with teachers, researchers and educationalists. In each chapter we have tried to make sure that readers have the opportunity to examine the quantitative and, where applicable, the qualitative research findings, as well as to weigh up the arguments and opinions that we offer.

An important extra dimension to our work is that it allows comparison of reading habits over time. The empirical research we conducted in 1994/5 repeated work carried out by Frank Whitehead and a team of researchers at the University of Sheffield in the 1970s. We were inspired to take on the project because of the quality of this original work, the results of which are still being widely referred to over two decades after they were first reported. We constructed our questionnaire to reflect the questions and format of the original; we chose the sample of children in a way that would allow us to generalise from our findings and allow comparisons to be drawn with the reading habits of children in the 1970s. In the appendix of this book we report the *Children's Reading Choices* project procedures in detail, and reproduce the questionnaire.

We did not simply reproduce the questionnaire devised by the Sheffield team in the 1970s. We wanted to investigate current concerns about the relationship between reading and the use of computers, about book and magazine purchasing patterns, about the influence of family reading habits on individual children. We wanted information on the reading experiences of children for whom English is not their first or sole language. We wanted to draw from our data some conclusions about patterns related to gender, class and ethnicity. We therefore designed the questionnaire to elicit as much of this information as possible whilst retaining the two basic objectives we had set ourselves: to provide a snapshot of children's reading at a particular moment, and to identify trends in children's reading over the period of two decades.

We were able to conduct the questionnaire survey because of the generosity of two sets of people. W. H. Smith PLC, the bookseller, sponsored the project, and staff from the company offered practical support and advice which demonstrated at every turn their enthusiasm to promote children's reading, their detailed knowledge of the field and their readiness to think creatively about young people's literacy. We would not have been able to conduct the survey without the support of teachers. Almost every school we approached from the sample we had constructed agreed to participate in the project. Individual teachers were assiduous in administering the survey – setting the tone to make sure that children took it seriously, keeping to the rather strict procedures which guaranteed to the children that their responses were confidential and would not be seen by their teachers, helping children who might have difficulties in understanding the format or language of the questionnaire. Teachers were generally interested in the work we were doing and were willing to put themselves out to return bundles of questionnaires and interrupt their lesson plans for the day. We distributed nearly 9,000 questionnaires and received a remarkably high return rate of 89 per cent – 7,976 questionnaires in all.

The second phase of the *Children's Reading Choices* project involved follow-up interviews with children in different parts of England. Again we are indebted to teachers, who made arrangements that allowed our interviewer, Paula Bryant, to hold discussions with children in quiet areas of their schools. In all, 87 interviews were tape-recorded and then analysed. The interviews took place in the summer term of 1995. The interview procedures and sample construction are detailed in the appendix of this book.

The third phase of the project has been the analysis and interpretation of the enormous amount of data that was yielded by the first two phases. This has involved the dissemination of the main findings and a great deal of discussion of the implications of what we have found. This book contributes to but does not, we hope, conclude that phase of the work.

The book consists of eight chapters which represent the major areas of our analysis and interpretation. In the first chapter we consider children's reading at different ages, and in doing so introduce some of the systems of classification used in the analysis. In Chapter 2 we report on children's favourite books and authors, concluding the chapter with a brief discussion on the appeal of Roald Dahl and Enid Blyton. In Chapter 3 we consider the importance of magazines, newspapers and comics to children's reading, and we draw upon the interview as well as the questionnaire findings. This chapter concludes with a discussion of teenage magazines and an analysis of one edition of the most popular magazine in our survey. Chapter 4 is concerned with girls' and boys' reading preferences and habits. We draw upon qualitative and quantitative data, and end with a discussion about gender, reading development and school. In Chapter 5 we report the survey findings on socio-economic background, ethnicity and reading preferences and consider the evidence about the influence upon children of family reading habits. Chapter 6, on children's reading habits, is about library use, book purchase and the influence of book ownership on reading patterns. Chapter 7 reports the findings on television viewing, computer use and reading the evening before the survey; the discussion in the Endpiece to the chapter raises points about the relationship between literacy and the different media. The final chapter is about changes in reading habits since the Whitehead survey in the 1970s. It concludes with some recommendations, and a discussion about the thorny issue of judging quality in children's reading material. The appendices contain the questionnaire and project procedures.

In each chapter we have attempted to report the findings clearly, to analyse the data and then to raise further questions and suggest lines of argument. We have added an Endpiece to five of the chapters: a discussion related to the main topic of the chapter, but expressing personal views and opinions rather than direct analysis or interpretation of the research findings. We hope that the format we have chosen will allow readers to dip into those topics which relate to their own interests and concerns, and to use this book to stimulate discussion. If we are to understand and prepare children for the literacy demands of the future we need hard information and wide-ranging debate; we need to know what children actually do read rather than what we wish they would read. We hope that *Children's Reading Choices* will make a useful contribution to understanding these complex literacy issues.

Christine Hall and **Martin Coles**,
The University of Nottingham, 1998

Acknowledgements

Our thanks go to:

- W. H. Smith for financial support and continued interest in the project;
- Mick Youngman for the sample design and advice;
- Jane Restorick for statistical advice and support;
- Val Fraser and Paula Bryant for their important contributions to the work of the project team;
- all the teachers and pupils who participated in the research.

Chapter 1

Reading at different ages

In this chapter, we establish that reading remains a very significant leisure time activity for children at 10, 12 and 14. We report findings about the amount of reading children report; the types of books which are most widely read, and the range and diversity of individuals' reading choices. In doing this, we explain some of the systems of categorising data collected in the *Children's Reading Choices* project. We go on to report information on the re-reading of books and numbers of books left unfinished. We conclude with the children's views of reading, their views of their own abilities as readers and a report of reading behaviours on a randomly chosen weekday evening.

The *Children's Reading Choices* project surveyed the reading habits of children aged 10, 12 and 14 during October 1994. There were approximately 2,500 children in each of the cohorts of 12- and 14-year-olds, and rather more (some 2,900) 10-year-olds. Generally, the youngest group were still in primary schools whereas the older groups of children were in secondary education.

Reading in the four weeks prior to the survey

Early in the questionnaire children were asked 'Have you read a book (or books) in the last four weeks?' In order to try to focus attention on voluntary, out-of-school reading, this was followed by the instruction 'Don't count books which a teacher said you must read as part of a lesson or for homework.' Teachers administering the questionnaire were asked to mention a local or national event which would help the pupils define the four-week period in question. For many children this would have been the beginning of the new school year.

The responses to this question, set out in Table 1.1, show a clear trend towards fewer books being read as children grow older. This finding is confirmed in other ways by the survey data.

Table 1.1 Reading of any book in the previous
month by age

Age	% 'yes' responses
10+	91.3
12+	80.5
14+	64.3

The question which followed asked children to record the titles of the books they had read during the four weeks prior to the survey. Again, the children were reminded about recording voluntary rather than school-required reading. Up to thirteen spaces were allowed for noting down titles. Of the 7,976 respondents, three cited thirteen books, filling all the spaces. The average number of books cited for the month, across all age groups, was 2.52.

These bald figures are, of course, potentially misleading. Children who have not read books might well have been reading other kinds of texts, including newspapers and magazines. The average number of books read carries with it no indication of the length or complexity of the books in question. Nevertheless, the comparison with (equally bald) figures in Whitehead's study is interesting (Whitehead *et al.*, 1977). The average number of books read by children in the four weeks prior to his 1971 survey was 2.39. The comparative figures are shown in Table 1.2.

The significant differences between the findings for the different cohorts relate to 10 year olds of both sexes and 12-year-old girls, where the amount of reading seems to have increased over the two decades between the surveys. There is also a significant decline in numbers of books read by 14-year-old boys. Other differences are not statistically significant.[1]

These findings can be interpreted as generally encouraging. Popular fears that the increase in other distractions for children in the 1990s has led to an overall decline in the amount of book reading might seem, on these figures, to be unfounded. Certainly, when the main findings from The *Children's Reading Choices* project were first disseminated, the press in England used these figures to announce a 'good news' story, under

Table 1.2 Average number of books read in one month, 1971 and 1994

Age	Boys, 1971	Boys, 1994	Girls, 1971	Girls, 1994
10+	2.68	2.98	3.28	3.71
12+	1.99	1.90	2.48	2.93
14+	1.78	1.45	2.15	2.06

Partial source: Whitehead *et al.*, 1977, p. 51

headlines such as 'Written Word keeps Appeal' (*Doncaster Evening Post*, 13.3.96) and 'TV Fails to Break Reading Habit' (*Daily Telegraph*, 11.3.96). Such stories, of course, become newsworthy only in the context of widespread belief that amounts and standards of reading are in decline.

The trend towards reading fewer books with age is noteworthy but not new. Whitehead *et al*. remarked in 1977: 'What is certainly worrying is the marked swing away from book reading as children grow older' (p. 272). It is also worth noting from the 1994 findings that, for boys, a statistically significant increase in reading between the two surveys at 10 years old becomes neutral at 12, and a significant decrease at 14. For girls a statistically significant increase at the ages of 10 and 12 becomes neutral at 14. One way of interpreting these figures would be to suggest that primary schools in England are more successful in promoting reading than they were in the 1970s. It might also be that in reading fewer books as they grow older, children are adopting more 'adult' patterns of reading, insofar as most adults probably read fewer than 2.52 books per month.

Range and diversity in children's reading

As might be expected, the range and diversity of books children read increase as they grow older. Again, this might be seen as reflecting increasingly adult reading patterns. This trend, and the complicating factor of girls' preferences for reading series titles such as *Point Horror* or *Sweet Valley High* are discussed more fully in chapters which follow. The diversity and eclecticism of children's reading habits struck us immediately as we read through the questionnaires; Whitehead too discusses 'the extraordinary diversity of book reading undertaken by these children' (p. 279).

We decided, on receiving the questionnaires, that we would begin our analysis by creating one very long book list, detailing every title and author that each child had mentioned. We would then be able to count multiple mentions of particular titles, and perhaps track down some of the more oddly ascribed authors and decode some of the more bizarre spellings of book titles. The final book list was daunting in size – 19,344 items long – but we were able to sort it alphabetically, count multiple mentions and re-ascribe authors where children had remembered wrongly. We then set about categorising the book list into units that seemed to reflect children's own patterns of choice.

We wanted to use the book list to consider the types of subjects that interested the children. It seemed to us that subject matter is central to the choice of book a child makes, and this judgement was confirmed by the interview phase of the work. The books on the list often fell into broad genre-related headings, for example, horror/ghost, science fiction/ fantasy. We considered how best to approach the categorisation of fiction and non-fiction texts. We could see from our initial consideration of the whole book list that children who were, for example, interested in horses would be likely to read both fiction and non-fiction that were clearly horse related. In the end, we decided that since we were interested in subject matter that attracted different children into reading, we would group non-fiction and fiction, 'high' culture and 'popular' culture together under category headings that reflected the subject matter of the texts. We therefore grouped the books that the children reported reading under fourteen different category headings.

We worked from the book list to try to create coherent categories that would be inclusive. We grouped horror and ghost stories together; similarly, science fiction and fantasy, crime and detective, and war and spy stories. We created separate categories for school-related books, sports-related books and animal-related books. We gave poetry books a separate category because we were interested in identifying which children were reading poetry. We grouped joke books, annuals, comic books and humour (often TV related) under the heading of comedy. A clearly important area of young people's reading relates to stories and information about growing up, and we decided on a single category to include romances, stories of relationships and teenage development (for example, Judy Blume's novels) and manuals about sex education or advice to teenagers. We created one category called 'Adventure', which included a great number of children's books (notably, the work of Enid Blyton and much by Roald Dahl) but which we extended to include works in which we judged that action was a prime feature. 'Adventure' therefore includes picaresque and quest novels and accounts of real life adventures and explorations. We needed some 'dump' categories and created three to attempt to draw out some distinctions. These were 'Other Non-Fiction' for those non-fiction texts which did not fit the subject categories, 'Other Fiction intended for Children/Teenagers' and an 'Unclassifiable' category. The coders' working definitions of the categories are included in the appendix to this book.

It will be immediately apparent that the allocation of books to these categories could not be a completely exact science. We operated according to the rule that subject matter took precedence over the text form, except in the case of poetry. So an adventure story about animals or school was placed in the animal-related or school category. To keep the practice as consistent as possible only three of the project team members coded the entire book list. All three of us have been English teachers in school; we teach in the area of children's literature and we are representative of both primary and secondary phases of education. We spent many hours coding the list together, to iron out as many difficulties as possible. As a check on the reliability of the coding, initially we each coded the same 3,000 items and corrected any discrepancies in the small number of cases where they occurred. We made extensive use of Nottingham University library's copy of the 'Global Books in Print' CD ROM to track down individual titles and series. W. H. Smith PLC gave us practical support in this work. Local children's librarians were extremely patient with us and generous in their willingness to share their expertise. A further check arose from the re-ordering of the whole book list once the codes had been entered on the computer.

The decision to categorise the book list in this way led, of course, to very broad selections of books within each category. The 'Animal Related' category, for example, contains *Black Beauty*, the *Saddle Club* series, George Orwell's *Animal Farm*, books on how to care for pets and diagnose their ailments, and *The Animals of Farthing Wood*.

What, then, do these categories demonstrate about children's reading at different ages? Tastes change as children get older, but some book types are read fairly consistently across the three ages covered by the survey. A similar percentage of children in each age group read horror/ghost and war/spy-related books. More 10-year-old pupils read science fiction/fantasy than other year groups, but the pattern is fairly even. Readers of crime and detective works are spread fairly evenly across the ages, with a slight dip in the 12-year-old range.

Adventure is overwhelmingly the most popular category for 10-year-old readers. An interest in books about animals is also very strong in 10-year-olds; this declines considerably as the children grow older. Since this category contains books with animals as main characters, the heavy weighting towards the younger age group is perhaps unsurprising. Horror and ghost, romance and relationships, science fiction and then comedy follow in order as preferences. More than 5 per cent of 10-year-olds choose to read poetry.

More 10-year-olds than 12- or 14-year-olds read school- and sports-related books. As children grow older their taste for reading these books diminishes; this is perhaps accounted for in part by the fact that most Year 6 pupils in England are in their final year of primary school awaiting transition to secondary school. School stories perhaps have a particular interest at this point, and sports are often also an important element, especially for boys, in the transition process and the establishing of new friends and particular identities.

Twelve-year-old children retain some of the younger children's appetite for adventure books, but are reading horror/ghost, romance/ relationships and science fiction books in proportions that are similar to the older age group. The reading of books in the 'comedy' category also declines steadily with age. Annuals, joke and comic books, included in this category, tend to be targeted at the younger age groups which would in part account for this decline. The poetry reading figures relating to age show an enthusiasm for reading poetry in 10-year-olds which has declined

Table 1.3 Reading of book types within each age group

Book type	% age 10+ having read a book in this category in the last 4 weeks	% age 12+ having read a book in this category in the last 4 weeks	% age 14+ having read a book in this category in the last 4 weeks
Adventure	65.8	39.2	19.3
Horror/ghost	18.0	23.4	22.1
Romance/ relationships	15.6	22.5	20.9
Animal related	33.0	11.8	5.6
Sci-fi/fantasy	13.1	12.3	11.9
Comedy	11.5	7.2	4.4
Crime/detective	5.9	4.6	6.3
Sports related	7.1	4.9	2.2
School	7.9	4.1	1.6
War/spy related	2.8	3.7	3.3
Poetry	5.6	1.9	0.3
Other non-fiction	8.5	6.4	5.8
Other fiction intended for children/teenagers	5.3	2.4	1.6
Unclassifiable	3.4	2.4	2.5

Table 1.4 Reading of book types across age groups

Book type	% readers aged 10+	% readers aged 12+	% readers aged 14+	Total
Adventure	57.2	28.1	14.7	100
Horror/ghost	31.8	34.0	34.2	100
Romance/ relationships	29.8	35.4	34.8	100
Animal related	69.3	20.5	10.2	100
Sci-fi/fantasy	39.0	30.2	30.8	100
Comedy	54.1	27.9	17.9	99
Crime/detective	38.7	25.0	36.3	100
Sports related	54.0	31.1	14.9	100
School	62.2	26.7	11.1	100
War/spy related	32.0	35.3	32.8	100.1
Poetry	75.2	21.4	3.4	100
Other non-fiction	44.3	27.7	27.9	99.9
Other fiction intended for children/teenagers	60.8	23.3	15.8	99.9
Unclassifiable	44.6	26.3	29.1	100

sharply by 12 and has all but disappeared by 14. Readers at 14 have a fairly evenly balanced diet of adventure, horror/ghost and books on romance and relationships. There is a readership for science fiction and fantasy, but then a much smaller percentage of children at this age who read crime and detective and animal-related books. Tables 1.3 and 1.4 set out this information.

Types of reader

In order to investigate further the diversity of individual children's reading habits, we decided to categorise the readers themselves into broad types. Whitehead in the original 1971 survey had attempted such a classification, into five categories: non-book reader, reader of narrative only, reader of non-narrative only, reader of both, and an unclassifiable category. His team found that narrative accounted for the overwhelming majority of children's reading at all three ages ('at least 77 % of the reading of the sample' p. 114), and that the proportions remained steady from 10 through to 12 and 14. Where 'non-narrative' was being read it was predominantly by boys, in a pattern which was also consistent across the ages.

We considered using the same system of classification, but an aspect of the eclecticism of individual children's reading lists made us decide to look at things differently. Reading through children's entries on their questionnaires, it was impossible not to be struck by the sophisticated 'adult' nature of some of the texts they were citing, alongside texts for young children which many had probably first encountered in their infancy. One pupil mentioned *The Beginner's Guide to Feminism* alongside *Cinderella*; another *The Rabbit's New Home* alongside a Stephen King horror novel. It seemed to us that these lists revealed a simple but important point about children's reading habits: that different books fulfil very different purposes for children and that they are used in different ways – to comfort, to excite, to inform, to relax with.

We devised a classification system which would help us consider the nature of children's eclectic tastes. The categories we decided upon were these:

- reader solely of children's fiction;
- reader solely of adult fiction;
- reader solely of non-fiction;
- 'hybrid' reader, i.e. a reader of books from more than one category;
- unclassifiable, including children who had not read a book in the previous four weeks.

(Fuller definitions are given in the appendix to the book.)

Again, of course, caveats are necessary. There is no clear and easy dividing line between 'children's fiction' and 'adult fiction'- good fiction is good fiction across age divisions. We are aware that in operating with these categories we are opening up long-standing and complex debates about the notion of audience within fiction written for even the youngest of children. There are no hard and fast distinctions to be drawn; and, indeed, a similar set of arguments holds true for fiction and non-fiction. How far is biographical or autobiographical work fictional?

On the other hand, it is interesting to know what proportion of 10-year-olds are reading only books which are marketed for adult readers, with all the attendant expectations of broader understanding of moral or ethical issues. It is interesting to know what proportion of children are reading only books which might be classified as non-fiction. So we agreed our classification system and did our best to ensure consistency between the three coders. We followed the procedures described above with relation to book type categories and coded 'Reader Type' and 'Book Type' at the same time. In deciding upon the children's or adults' fiction categories, we considered where possible the marketing of the books and what that indicated about the expected readership. Books marketed for younger teenage children were put in the children's fiction category; books marketed for older teenagers as well as adults (for example, Terry Pratchett's or Sue Townsend's books) were put into the adult fiction category. We included the distinction between fiction and non-fiction readers because we wanted to consider the percentage of children who read only one or the other, particularly in relation to the often quoted idea that many boys tend to read only non-fiction.

Table 1.5 shows percentages of children who fall into each of the reader type categories. These figures show the overwhelming popularity of children's and teenage fiction as a reading diet for 10–14-year-olds. A sizeable proportion of children read only what might be considered 'adult' fiction; the percentage perhaps seems appropriate to the numbers of sophisticated and able readers who are likely to be included in a cross-section of this size. The figure of nearly 16 per cent of the children who were reading across our categories – reading 'children's' and 'adult' fiction, reading non-fiction and fiction – is an indication of the range and variety of children's reading patterns which struck us so forcibly as we read through their questionnaires. The small percentage (2.8 per cent) of children who read only non-fiction is also interesting, particularly in the light of much popular wisdom that suggests that boys at these ages are turning away from fiction to an exclusive diet of non-fiction. Children who read at these ages read predominantly fiction; when they read non-fiction it is most likely to be alongside works of fiction.

Related to age, the figures in Table 1.6 show, as one would expect, a greater preponderance of readers solely of children's and teenage fiction

Table 1.5 Reader types

Reader type	% of sample
Children's fiction	50.5
Adult fiction	10.2
Non-fiction	2.8
Hybrid	15.8
Unclassifiable	20.7
Total	100.0

Table 1.6 Reader types by age

Reader type	% aged 10+	% aged 12+	% aged 14+	Total
Children's fiction	51.0	33.1	15.9	100
Adult fiction	6.5	19.7	73.8	100
Non-fiction	24.2	41.2	34.6	100
Hybrid	43.2	29.7	27.1	100

in the youngest age group, diminishing as the children grow older. Similarly, readers of adult fiction come predominantly from the oldest age category. There are very few 10-year-olds reading exclusively adult fiction, although a good many of them are dipping into non-fiction and the occasional adult title. Similarly, there are 14-year-olds enjoying titles which might seem relatively young for them. These are transitional years for children in all sorts of ways – in terms of schooling and their sense of their own identities in relation to themselves and to others. The eclecticism and range of their reading within these categories seems likely to be helpful in making those transitions.

Re-reading and leaving books unfinished

The children were asked to identify which of the books they reported reading in the four weeks prior to the survey were ones that they had read before, and which books they had decided to leave unfinished. It is striking that one third (33.2 per cent) of the children had re-read one or more books in the previous month. Five per cent of children had re-read three or more books. The trend is for younger children and girls to re-read most.

This is similar to the trend the Whitehead team found in the 1970s. They noted a steady decrease in the absolute number of re-readings with increasing age, but noted a tendency for 12-year-olds to re-read, which

Table 1.7 Re-reading by age

Number of books re-read	% aged 10+	% aged 12+	% aged 14+	Total
0	32.6	30.1	37.3	100
1	41.0	32.7	26.3	100
2	44.8	34.5	20.7	100
3	52.3	28.0	19.7	100

they suggested might be associated with children 'cling[ing] to their juvenile narrative reading, while at the same time experimenting to a modest but increasing extent with adult narrative books' (p. 146). Our interpretation is similar and relates to the previous discussion about the eclectic nature of children's reading and the variety of purposes any one child might have for reading. Re-reading a familiar story creates a bridge back to an earlier experience. For a younger child, the re-reading might take the form of an independent reading as opposed to an earlier shared experience of listening to a story. Clearly, a re-reading is a differently structured kind of reading experience to an initial reading, and will have different implications, since the choice is made with prior knowledge of the book rather than in anticipation of what the book might offer. Our view is that this is an aspect of children's reading behaviours which merits closer attention. Table 1.7, which needs to be approached cautiously because of the decline in the amount of reading in the older age categories, nevertheless gives an indication of the pattern of re-reading related to age.

Fewer children had left a book unfinished in the four weeks prior to the survey than had re-read a book. Approximately 19 per cent of pupils in the survey had left 1, 2, or 3 books unfinished. Generally, children who read most (girls and younger children) are more likely to be re-reading and to be leaving books unfinished. Twelve-year-olds in the survey left fewest books unfinished; the most likely types of books to be unfinished are those which are most widely read, as would be expected. Again, the patterns appear to have remained similar over the last three decades since Whitehead reports similar findings.

Views of reading at different ages

Respondents to the questionnaire were asked to complete this sentence with one or two words: 'I think that reading is . . . ' The responses were coded as follows (see Table 1.8):

   (i)   positive responses, e.g., 'very good', 'brilliant', 'excellent', 'fun';
  (ii) neutral responses, e.g., 'all right', 'OK';

   (iii) negative responses, e.g., 'boring', 'dull';
   (iv) education-related responses, e.g., 'helps with other work';
    (v) leisure-related responses, e.g., 'relaxing';
   (vi) responses which compared reading unfavourably with television;
  (vii) unclassifiable.

Table 1.8 Children's views of reading

Category of response	% of sample
(i) Positive	53.0
(ii) Neutral	24.3
(iii) Negative	9.6
(iv) Educational	8.2
(v) Leisure	4.1
(vi) Compared with television	0.1
(vii) Unclassifiable	0.7
Total	100

Almost all (97.9 per cent) of the sample completed this question. The overwhelming majority of responses fell into the 'positive' or 'neutral' categories.

If we consider categories (i), (iv) and (v) together, then 65.3 per cent view reading in a positive light. Many of the positive comments referred to the fun of reading, for example, common responses were 'enjoyable and fun', 'great fun and relaxing', 'fun and interesting and exciting'. Other respondents noted the privacy reading allows them: 'pretty good when I am alone and can read without being interrupted by anybody'. Some children alluded to the escapist element of private reading: 'prite good because it sort of a spechiel world in your room [sic]'; 'good and taking you into different places'; 'an amazing and wonderful chance to explore other worlds'. Some respondents made the distinction between reading for their own pleasure and reading for school or other purposes: 'good, just as long as no-one is makeing [sic] me do it. I like reading at my own pace when I choose to'.

Of the negative responses, some children found reading an un-interesting or tedious activity:

'boring' was the most common of these descriptors ('sometimes boring', 'quite boring', 'slightly boring', 'very boring', 'really boring', 'absolutely boring', 'totally boring'). Other negative responses implied a lot of effort which was 'not worth it', or included references to a perceived lack of ability: 'boring (very) because I can not read'.

Of the responses that were categorised as educational or instructive, respondents noted the particular uses of reading to their lives: 'it helps you to explain and talk to people'; 'you learn a lot and it helps you find out about real life'; 'a way to help your english' [*sic*]; 'important for us to learn new words'; 'very important to increase your vocabulary'; 'it helps your spelling'. Those who saw reading as more of a leisure pursuit commented that it was 'a helpful pastime and hobby'; 'a good way to pass the time'; 'relaxing'; 'calming'; 'a good thig it cheers me up when I Bord' [*sic*].

The younger children tended to judge reading more positively than the older ones did. Combining categories (i, iv and v), 77 per cent of 10-year-olds, 60 per cent of 12-year-olds and 57 per cent of 14-year-olds gave positive responses (see Table 1.9).

Table 1.9 Children's views of reading by age

Age	Positive (%)	Neutral (%)	Negative (%)	Educational (%)	Good pastime (%)	Category vi & vii (%)	Total
10+	71.1	18.3	4.3	4.6	1.6	0.3	100.2
12+	48.3	28.7	10.7	7.9	4.0	0.5	100.1
14+	37.4	26.9	14.7	12.5	7.2	1.3	100

Older children were more likely to phrase their positive answers in terms of the educational and instructive benefits of reading than younger children, and were more likely to view reading as a good pastime. This no doubt reflects the increasing pressures of school work as public examinations draw nearer for 14-year-olds, and perhaps also a more adult concept of 'pastimes' and hobbies. Girls responded more positively than boys. Of all girls, 73.5 per cent viewed reading positively compared to 57.5 per cent of all boys. Girls are more likely to see the educational benefits of reading than boys and also more likely to think that reading is a good pastime. These attitudinal differences are discussed in greater depth in Chapter 4.

Children's views of themselves as readers

Children were asked 'About how much reading do you think you do?' Most children in the survey thought they did an average amount or 'quite a lot' of reading (see Table 1.10).

The proportions of children who see themselves as reading large amounts diminishes as the children grow older. This finding is, of course, based on the children's perceptions which may not be accurate. Indeed it is quite possible that the older children are being more realistic in their assessment of how much reading they do, rather than actually reading less. Nevertheless other data in the survey lends credence to the accuracy of children's perceptions. The 36 per cent of 14-year-olds who reported reading 'not very much' or 'only a little' approximates to the number who

Table 1.10 Children's perceptions of the amount they read

Amount of reading	% of total sample
A large amount	13.8
Quite a lot	24.5
About average	34.8
Not very much	18.8
Only a little	8.1
Total	100

Table 1.11 Children's perceptions of the amount they read by age

Amount of reading	% 10+	% 12+	% 14+
A large amount	18.5	12.7	9.9
Quite a lot	28.3	24.5	20.1
About average	35.3	34.7	34.1
Not very much	13.3	18.8	25.0
Only a little	4.6	9.3	11.0
Total	100	100	100.1

Table 1.12 Children's perceptions of their own reading abilities

View of reading ability	% of sample
Very good	21.1
Good	38.0
Average	31.3
Not very good	7.8
Poor	1.8
Total	100

had not read a book in the four weeks prior to the survey. The results according to the age groupings are given in Table 1.11.

The respondents were also asked 'Do you think you are good at reading?' Children at all three ages generally consider themselves to be good at reading. Over 59 per cent of the children thought they were 'good' or 'very good' at reading; only 9.6 per cent thought they were 'not very good' or 'poor' (see Table 1.12).

A consistent pattern of responses emerges over the three different age groups, particularly in relation to those who consider themselves less able readers (Table 1.13). Over 90 per cent of pupils in each age group consider themselves average or better readers, although older children are less likely than younger ones to claim that they are 'very good' readers. This perhaps reflects a more technicist view of reading – being able to decode print efficiently – amongst younger readers, and a broader view of

Table 1.13 Children's perceptions of their own reading abilities by age

View of reading ability	% 10+	% 12+	% 14+
Very good	25.1	20.7	17.2
Good	38.3	38.0	37.8
Average	27.2	31.5	35.8
Not very good	8.1	7.9	7.1
Poor	1.2	2.0	2.1
Total	99.9	100.1	100

reading amongst teenagers. Nevertheless, it is heartening to note the confidence that children display in their reading abilities; particularly if one accepts the argument that children with low self-esteem as readers are less likely to read, and are therefore more likely to exacerbate any difficulties or sense of failure they might be experiencing.

One evening's reading

Respondents were asked 'Did you do any reading last night?' (Table 1.14). If their answer was positive they were then asked to specify how long they had spent reading (Table 1.15). Two-thirds of the sample (65 per cent) reported doing some reading during the previous evening.

Younger children were more likely to report reading during the

Table 1.14 Amount of reading reported in one evening

Time	% of sample
No time	35.0
Up to 0.5 hour	26.5
0.5–1.5 hours	28.7
1.5–2.5 hours	6.1
2.5–3.5 hours	2.3
More than 3.5 hours	1.4
Total	100

Table 1.15 Amount of reading reported in one evening by % age

Age	No time	Less than 0.5 hours	0.5–1.5 hours	1.5–2.5 hours	2.5–3.5 hours	More than 3.5 hours
10+	30.0	29.4	28.4	7.1	2.9	2.2
12+	36.4	24.0	29.2	6.8	2.4	1.2
14+	39.0	25.6	28.8	4.5	1.6	0.6

evening before the survey. They were also more likely to report having read for longer periods of time. Clearly, self-reported lengths of time spent on an activity are likely to be unreliable, particularly amongst younger children whose conception of time passing might be more than usually subjective. It is difficult for readers of any age to track the passing of time accurately if they are absorbed in a book. However, the pattern is consistent with the general findings reported in this chapter: of those children who reported that they had not read at all, the largest percentage was of 14-year-olds. Amongst 10-year-old children, 12.2 per cent reported that they had read for at least one and a half hours in the previous evening, whereas for 12-year-olds this figure is 10.4 per cent, and for 14-year-olds it is 6.7 per cent.

Summary

- Children tend to read fewer books as they grow older.
- In the *Children's Reading Choices* survey, the average number of books read in the month prior to the survey, across all age groups, was 2.52. The average number of books read by children in the four weeks prior to the 1971 survey was 2.39.
- These figures indicate a slight, but statistically significant, increase in the amount of reading done by 10-year-olds of both sexes and 12-year-old girls over the two decades between the surveys. There is a significant decline in numbers of books read by 14-year-old boys.
- Children at the ages of 10, 12 and 14 read a wide range of books. They are highly eclectic in their reading habits.
- Strongly plotted 'adventure' stories are very popular across the ages.
- There is a declining interest in school-, animal- and sports-related stories and in books within the 'comedy' category after the age of 10.
- A minority taste for science fiction, horror and ghost stories, war- and spy-related books, and crime and detection is sustained fairly consistently across the age range.
- Children are increasingly interested in books about romance and relationships as they grow older.
- More than 5 per cent of 10-year-olds choose to read poetry, but this interest in poetry is not sustained, and has all but disappeared in 14-year-olds.
- Only a small percentage (2.8 per cent) of children are exclusively readers of non-fiction. Children at these ages read predominantly fiction; when they read non-fiction it is most likely to be alongside works of fiction.
- Children between 10 and 14 are generally reading books which have been marketed as children's or teenage fiction. About 10 per cent of children are reading only books which are marketed for adults, but

these readers are largely 14-year-olds.

- Nearly 16 per cent of the children surveyed were reading a mixture of 'children's' and 'adult' fiction and non-fiction in the month before the survey. There was a notable range in the genres of text and in levels of sophistication and complexity within individual children's reading choices.

- One-third of the children had re-read one or more books in the previous month. Five per cent of children had re-read three or more books. The trend is for younger children and girls to re-read most.

- Most children respond positively when asked their views of reading. Fewer than 10 per cent responded negatively.

- Most children, when asked, think that they do an average amount or 'quite a lot' of reading. However, 36 per cent of 14-year-olds report that they read 'not very much' or 'only a little.'

- Children at all three ages generally consider themselves to be good at reading. About two-thirds of children think they are 'good' or 'very good' at reading. Less than one-tenth think that they are 'not very good' or 'poor'.

- Two-thirds of the children reported doing some reading during the evening before the survey. Younger children spend more of their leisure time reading than older children do.

Note

1. A 'T-test' was conducted to test the significances of the differences between the mean scores. Since the standard deviation for the 1971 survey sample groups was unknown it was assumed, for the sake of this exercise, to be the same as that in the 1994 survey groups. There were highly significant differences ($p < 0.01$) for 10+ boys, 10+ girls, and 12+ girls where the number of books read has increased in the two decades between the surveys. There was also a highly significant difference ($p < 0.01$) in the figures for 14+ boys where the number of books read has decreased. Differences in the figures for 12+ boys and 14+ girls were not statistically significant.

Chapter 2

Favourite books

In this chapter, we report the titles of the books which children at 10, 12 and 14 had been reading in the four weeks prior to the survey. We consider the book lists in relation to the age and sex of the children, and consider the importance of series books to children's leisure-time reading. Children were also asked to name their favourite authors. These findings are reported and compared to the 1971 findings. Finally we consider how the findings on the age, sex, class and ethnicity of the respondents relates to their choice of a favourite author or series. A brief discussion on the appeal of Roald Dahl and Enid Blyton, the most popular individual authors, concludes the chapter.

Favourite titles

Children were asked to list the titles and authors of the books they had been reading in the four weeks prior to the survey. The information they returned was not always easy to process. Sometimes we had problems with the legibility of the writing or the eccentric spellings, although this was a very minor problem. Sometimes authors had been wrongly ascribed to texts (for example, several children thought that Enid Blyton had written *What Katy Did*). Again, this was a minor problem; when the child's intention was clear the correct author could be ascribed. More problematic, from our point of view, was the fact that many children mentioned books which were part of a series without giving the specific title they had been reading. Many children wrote entries such as *Babysitters Club* or *Secret Seven*, generic titles which could refer to a relatively large number of individual novels. Other children mentioned the name of the protagonist – Adrian Mole, for example, which could refer to several of Sue Townsend's books.

We describe, in Chapter 1, the decision to create a book list of the 19,344 titles and then to reorder the list, count the duplicate entries and relate the findings to the different variables of age, sex and social background. The popularity of what we will call 'series books' complicates the reporting.

We use the term 'series books' as a shorthand to refer both to those books marketed under a generic title, such as *Point Horror*, *The Famous Five* or *Sweet Valley High* and also to novels with sequels, such as *The Secret Diary of Adrian Mole*, and to novels most often known to children under their popular media title, such as *Red Dwarf*. In some cases the individual titles of novels within a series appear to be well known to their readers (for example, children reading C. S. Lewis's *Narnia* sequence tended to know the individual titles); others, such as the *Asterix* and *Garfield* series tended to be referred to generically.

In reporting the children's favourite titles, then, we offer two lists for consideration. The first list is of the most frequently mentioned titles and series, with individual titles alongside references to series books. The second list contains only individual titles, whatever series they might, or might not, be in.

List 1: most frequently mentioned titles and series

50+ mentions

267	*The BFG*	Roald Dahl
235	*Matilda*	Roald Dahl
217	*The Witches*	Roald Dahl
212	*The Twits*	Roald Dahl
199	*The Famous Five*	Enid Blyton
197	*Charlie and the Chocolate Factory*	Roald Dahl
160	*Adrian Mole*	Sue Townsend
148	*Fantastic Mr Fox*	Roald Dahl
146	*James and the Giant Peach*	Roald Dahl
139	*The Babysitter I, II & III*	R. L. Stine
125	*Jurassic Park*	Michael Crichton
110	*George's Marvellous Medicine*	Roald Dahl
106	*The Hobbit*	J. R. R. Tolkien
93	*The Magic Finger*	Roald Dahl
93	*The Secret Garden*	Frances Hodgson Burnett
91	*The Secret Seven series*	Enid Blyton
80	*Babysitters Club series*	Ann M. Martin
78	*Boy*	Roald Dahl
75	*Garfield series*	Jim Davis
74	*Asterix series*	Rene Goscinny
69	*Sweet Valley High / Twins / University series*	Francine Pascal
66	*Red Dwarf series*	Grant Naylor
66	*The Lion, the Witch and the Wardrobe*	C. S. Lewis
63	*It*	Stephen King

62	*The Beano*	
59	*Trick or Treat*	R. Tankersley Cusick
58	*Forever*	Judy Blume
57	*Black Beauty*	Anna Sewell
54	*Dracula*	Bram Stoker
53	*Danny the Champion of the World*	Roald Dahl

20–50 mentions

48	*Superfudge*	Judy Blume
48	*Beach House*	R. L. Stine
47	*The Saddle Club* series	Bonnie Bryant
47	*The Animals of Farthingwood* series	Colin Dann
46	*Lord of the Rings*	J. R. R. Tolkien
46	*What Katy Did* series	Susan Coolidge
46	*Funhouse*	Diane Hoh
44	*Charlie and the Great Glass Elevator*	Roald Dahl
44	*Anastasia* series	Lois Lowry
43	*The Girlfriend*	R. L Stine
43	*The Borrowers*	Mary Norton
43	*The Boyfriend*	R. L. Stine
42	*April Fools*	R. Tankersley Cusick
42	*Beach Party*	R. L. Stine
41	*The Worst Witch* series	Jill Murphy
39	*Dream Date*	Sinclair Smith
38	*Point Horror* series	Various
37	*Turbulent Term of Tyke Tiler*	Gene Kemp
37	*The Wind in the Willows*	Kenneth Grahame
37	*The Accident*	Diane Hoh
36	*Esio Trot*	Roald Dahl
36	*Little Women*	Louisa May Alcott
36	*Teacher's Pet*	R. Tankersley Cusick
36	*Flowers in the Attic*	Virginia Andrews
36	*Hit and Run*	R. L. Stine
36	*Mr Majeika* series	Humphrey Carpenter
35	*Revolting Rhymes*	Roald Dahl
35	*The Iron Man*	Ted Hughes
32	*The Snowman*	R. L. Stine
32	*The Lifeguard*	R. Tankersley Cusick
32	*Alice in Wonderland*	Lewis Carroll
31	*Madam Doubtfire*	Anne Fine
30	*The Cemetery*	D. L. Athkins
30	*Alien*	Jane O' Brien
30	*Goosebumps* series	R. L. Stine

30	*The Invitation*	Diane Hoh
30	*The Train*	Diane Hoh
29	*Winnie the Pooh*	A. A. Milne
29	*The Railway Children*	Edith Nesbit
29	*The Dandy*	
29	*The Naughtiest Girl* series	Enid Blyton
29	*The Waitress*	Sinclair Smith
28	*Watership Down*	Richard Adams
28	*The Pet Cemetery*	Stephen King
28	*The Cheerleader*	Caroline Cooney
28	*Camp Fear*	Carol Ellis
27	*Tiger Eyes*	Judy Blume
27	*Going Solo*	Roald Dahl
27	*Are You There God, It's Me Margaret*	Judy Blume
27	*My Naughty Little Sister* series	Dorothy Edwards
27	*The Perfume*	Caroline Cooney
26	*Oliver Twist*	Charles Dickens
26	*Aladdin*	
26	*The Hitchhiker*	R. L. Stine
26	*Home Alone I & II*	Todd Stasser / A. L. Singer
26	*Sherlock Holmes* series	Sir Arthur Conan Doyle
25	*Jessica* series	Francine Pascal
25	*Diary of Anne Frank*	Anne Frank
25	*The Fever*	Diane Hoh
25	*Mother's Helper*	A. Bates
25	*Sonic the Hedgehog* series	Martin Adams
25	*Redwall* series	Brian Jacques
24	*Flat Stanley* series	Jeff Brown
24	*Guinness Book of Records*	
24	*Jungle Book*	Rudyard Kipling
24	*The Window*	Carol Ellis
24	*Room 13*	Robert Swindells
24	*Please Mrs Butler*	Allan Ahlberg
23	*Hallowe'en Party*	R. L. Stine
23	*Monty* series	Colin West
23	*The Dead Girlfriend*	R. L. Stine
23	*Charlotte's Web*	E. B. White
23	*Heidi*	Johanna Spyri
23	*The Rats*	James Herbert
22	*It Shouldn't Happen to a Vet* series	James Herriot
22	*Vlad the Drac* series	Ann Jungman
22	*Silence of the Lambs*	Thomas Harris
22	*Robin Hood*	
22	*Tales of a Fourth Grade Nothing*	Judy Blume

22	*Woof*	Allan Ahlberg
21	*The Client*	John Grisham
21	*Misery*	Stephen King
21	*Blubber*	Judy Blume
21	*Napper* series	Martin Waddell
21	*Treasure Island*	R. L. Stevenson
20	*Jill's Riding Club* series	Ruby Ferguson
20	*Biggles* series	W. E. Johns
20	*Deenie*	Judy Blume
20	*Dennis the Menace*	
20	*Hardy Boys* series	Franklin W. Dixon
20	*Just as Long as We're Together*	Judy Blume
20	*The Sheep-Pig*	Dick King-Smith
20	*Stig of the Dump*	Clive King
20	*Tintin* series	Hergé
20	*Take That*	
20	*101 Dalmations*	Dodie Smith

10–19 Mentions

19	*Goodnight Mr Tom*	Michelle Magorian
19	*Peter Pan*	J. M. Barrie
19	*Puzzle Adventure/Island* series	J. Tyler/G. Waters
19	*My Girl and My Girl II*	Patricia Hermes
19	*The Little Vampire*	Angela Sommer-Bodenburg
19	*The Hodgeheg*	Dick King-Smith
19	*Freeze Tag*	Caroline B. Cooney
19	*Freshman* series	Lynda A. Cooney
19	*The Dead Game*	A. Bates
19	*The Demon Headmaster*	Gillian Cross
19	*Sharpe's Company/Eagle* series	Bernard Cornwell
19	*Diary of a Teenage Health Freak*	Aidan Macfarlane and Ann McPherson
19	*Dilly the Dinosaur* series	Tony Bradman
19	*The Firm*	John Grisham
19	*Computer book*	Various
18	*The Silver Sword*	Ian Serraillier
18	*Where's Wally?* series	Martin Handford
18	*Shoot*	
18	*Poems*	Various
18	*Mallory Towers*	Enid Blyton
18	*Truckers*	Terry Pratchett
18	*The Wizard of Oz*	Frank L. Baum
18	*Flour Babies*	Anne Fine

18	*Dirty Beasts*	Roald Dahl
18	*Beethoven*	Robert Tine
18	*Mossflower*	Brian Jacques
17	*Paddington Bear* series	Michael Bond
17	*Mort*	Terry Pratchett
17	*Honey I Shrunk/Blew Up the Kids*	
17	*Goggle-Eyes*	Anne Fine
16	*Better than Life*	Rob Grant and Doug Naylor
16	*The Story of Tracey Beaker*	Jacqeline Wilson
16	*Mr Bean* series	R. Driscoll
16	*Call Waiting*	R. L. Stine
16	*Everyone Else's Parents Say Yes*	Paula Danzinger
15	*Kristy* series	Ann M. Martin
15	*Bravo Two Zero*	Andy McNabb
15	*Buddy*	Nigel Hinton
15	*The Vampire's Promise*	Caroline B. Cooney
15	*Dark Portal*	Robin Jarvis
15	*The Colour of Magic*	Terry Pratchett
15	*Heaven*	Virginia Andrews
14	*The Shining*	Stephen King
14	*Henry Sugar*	Roald Dahl
14	*Ramona*	Beverley Cleary
14	*White Fang*	Jack London
14	*Beauty and the Beast*	
14	*The Second World War*	
14	*Freckle Juice*	Judy Blume
14	*It's Not the End of the World*	Judy Blume
14	*The Phantom*	Christopher Pike
14	*13 Tales of Horror*	A. Finnis (ed.)
14	*Soccer at Sandford*	Rob Childs
14	*The Stranger*	Caroline B. Cooney
13	*There's an Awful Lot of Weirdos in Our Neighbourhood*	Colin McNaughton
13	*Stacey* series	Ann M. Martin
13	*Wuthering Heights*	Emily Brontë
13	*The Whitby Witches*	Robin Jarvis
13	*The Queen and I*	Sue Townsend
13	*The Playmate*	Herbert Richardson
13	*It's Not Fair*	Bel Mooney
13	*Jane Eyre*	Charlotte Brontë
13	*Animal Farm*	George Orwell
13	*Around the World in 80 Days*	Jules Vernes
13	*The Machine Gunners*	Robert Westall
13	*Martin's Mice*	Dick King-Smith

13	*The Pelican Brief*	John Grisham
13	*The Return of the Vampire*	Caroline B. Cooney
13	*The Mask*	Dean R. Koontz
13	*Bill's New Frock*	Anne Fine
13	*The Eighteenth Emergency*	Betsy Byars
13	*Frankenstein*	Mary Shelley
13	*Gremlins*	Angus McVicar
13	*Free Willy*	Nigel Robinson
12	*Gulliver's Travels*	Jonathan Swift
12	*I Was a Teenage Worrier*	Ross Asquith
12	*Mrs Pepperpot* series	Alf Prøysen
12	*Iggie's House*	Judy Blume
12	*Harry's Mad*	Dick King-Smith
12	*The Haunted House*	Jan Pienkowski
12	*The Enchanted Wood*	Enid Blyton
12	*Great Expectations*	Charles Dickens
12	*The Call of the Wild*	Jack London
12	*The Crystal Maze*	Peter Arnold
12	*Summer Dreams, Winter Love*	Mary Francis Shura
12	*Carrie's War*	Nina Bawden
12	*Batman*	
12	*Salamanastron*	Brian Jacques
12	*Kidnapped*	R. L. Stevenson
11	*Star Wars*	George Lucas
11	*The Light Fantastic*	Terry Pratchett
11	*Jack and the Beanstalk*	
11	*My Secret Admirer*	Carol Ellis
11	*The Reaper Man*	Terry Pratchett
11	*The Bible*	
11	*To Kill a Mockingbird*	Harper Lee
11	*Uncanny/Unreal*	Paul Jennings
11	*Agent Arthur* series	Usborne Publishing
11	*Carpet People*	Terry Pratchett
11	*Diggers*	Terry Pratchett
11	*Hitchhiker's Guide to the Galaxy*	Douglas Adams
11	*David Copperfield*	Charles Dickens
11	*The Magician's Nephew*	C. S. Lewis
11	*Manchester United*	
11	*One Nil*	Tony Bradman
11	*Pride and Prejudice*	Jane Austen
11	*The Snow Spider*	Jenny Nimmo
10	*Snow White*	
10	*The Owl Who Was Afraid of the Dark*	Jill Tomlinson
10	*Martin the Warrior*	Brian Jacques

10	*Heard It in the Playground*	Allan Ahlberg
10	*The Horse and His Boy*	C. S. Lewis
10	*Hound of the Baskervilles*	Sir Arthur Conan Doyle
10	*How Dogs Really Work*	Alan Snow
10	*The Magic Faraway Tree*	Enid Blyton
10	Funny stories	
10	*Conrad's War*	Andrew Davies
10	*Rhyme Stew*	Roald Dahl
10	*The Little Mermaid*	Hans Christian Andersen
10	*The Little Princess*	Frances Hodgson Burnett
10	*Lords and Ladies*	Terry Pratchett
10	*Petals on the Wind*	Virginia Andrews
10	*In the Pool*	Jan Ormerod

List 2: most frequently mentioned individual titles

50+ mentions

267	*The BFG*	Roald Dahl
235	*Matilda*	Roald Dahl
217	*The Witches*	Roald Dahl
212	*The Twits*	Roald Dahl
197	*Charlie and the Chocolate Factory*	Roald Dahl
148	*Fantastic Mr Fox*	Roald Dahl
146	*James and the Giant Peach*	Roald Dahl
125	*Jurassic Park*	Michael Crichton
110	*George's Marvellous Medicine*	Roald Dahl
106	*The Hobbit*	J. R. R. Tolkien
93	*The Magic Finger*	Roald Dahl
93	*The Secret Garden*	Frances Hodgson Burnett
78	*Boy*	Roald Dahl
66	*The Lion, the Witch and the Wardrobe*	C. S. Lewis
63	*It*	Stephen King
59	*Trick or Treat*	R. Tankersley Cusick
58	*Forever*	Judy Blume
57	*Black Beauty*	Anna Sewell
54	*Dracula*	Bram Stoker
53	*Danny the Champion of the World*	Roald Dahl

20–50 mentions

48	*Superfudge*	Judy Blume
48	*Beach House*	Bonnie Bryant
46	*Lord of the Rings*	J. R. R. Tolkien

46	*The Funhouse*	Diane Hoh
44	*Charlie and the Great Glass Elevator*	Roald Dahl
43	*The Girlfriend*	R. L. Stine
43	*The Borrowers*	Mary Norton
43	*The Boyfriend*	R. L. Stine
42	*April Fool*	R. Tankersley Cusick
42	*Beach Party*	R. L. Stine
39	*Dream Date*	Sinclair Smith
37	*The Turbulent Term of Tyke Tiler*	Gene Kemp
37	*The Wind in the Willows*	Kenneth Grahame
37	*The Accident*	Diane Hoh
36	*Esio Trot*	Roald Dahl
36	*Little Women*	Louisa May Alcott
36	*Teacher's Pet*	R. Tankersley Cusick
36	*Flowers in the Attic*	Virginia Andrews
36	*Hit and Run*	R. L. Stine
35	*Revolting Rhymes*	Roald Dahl
35	*The Iron Man*	Ted Hughes
32	*The Snowman*	R. L. Stine
32	*The Lifeguard*	Richie Tankersley Cusick
32	*Alice in Wonderland*	Lewis Carroll
31	*Madam Doubtfire*	Anne Fine
30	*The Cemetery*	D. L. Athkins
30	*Alien*	Jane O'Brien
30	*The Invitation*	Diane Hoh
30	*The Train*	Diane Hoh
29	*Winnie the Pooh*	A. A. Milne
29	*The Railway Children*	Edith Nesbitt
29	*The Waitress*	Sinclair Smith
28	*Watership Down*	Richard Adams
28	*The Pet Cemetery*	Stephen King
28	*The Cheerleader*	Caroline B. Cooney
28	*Camp Fear*	Carol Ellis
27	*Tiger Eyes*	Judy Blume
27	*Going Solo*	Roald Dahl
27	*Are You There God, It's Me Margaret*	Judy Blume
27	*My Naughty Little Sister*	Dorothy Edwards
27	*The Perfume*	Caroline B. Cooney
26	*Oliver Twist*	Charles Dickens
26	*Aladdin*	
26	*The Hitchhiker*	R. L. Stine
25	*Diary of Anne Frank*	Anne Frank
25	*The Fever*	Diane Hoh
25	*Mother's Helper*	A. Bates

24	*Flat Stanley*	Jeff Brown
24	*The Guinness Book of Records*	
24	*The Jungle Book*	Rudyard Kipling
24	*The Window*	Carol Ellis
24	*Room 13*	Robert Swindells
24	*Please Mrs Butler*	Allan Ahlberg
23	*Hallowe'en Party*	R. L. Stine
23	*The Dead Girlfriend*	R. L. Stine
23	*Charlotte's Web*	E. B. White
23	*Heidi*	Johanna Spyri
23	*The Rats*	James Herbert
22	*Silence of the Lambs*	Thomas Harris
22	*Robin Hood*	
22	*Tales of a Fourth Grade Nothing*	Judy Blume
22	*Woof*	Allan Ahlberg
21	*The Client*	John Grishan
21	*Misery*	Stephen King
21	*Blubber*	Judy Blume
21	*Treasure Island*	R. L. Stevenson
20	*Deenie*	Judy Blume
20	*Just as Long as We're Together*	Judy Blume
20	*The Sheep-Pig*	Dick King-Smith
20	*Stig of the Dump*	Clive King
20	*Take That*	
20	*101 Dalmations*	Dodie Smith

10–19 mentions

19	*Goodnight Mr Tom*	Michelle Magorian
19	*Peter Pan*	J. M. Barrie
19	*The Little Vampire*	A. Sommer-Bodenburg
19	*The Hodgeheg*	Dick King-Smith
19	*Freeze Tag*	Caroline B. Cooney
19	*The Dead Game*	A. Bates
19	*The Demon Headmaster*	Gillian Cross
19	*Diary of a Teenage Health Freak*	Aidan Macfarlane
19	*The Firm*	John Grisham
18	*The Silver Sword*	Ian Serraillier
18	*Truckers*	Terry Prachett
18	*The Wizard of Oz*	Frank L. Baum
18	*Flour Babies*	Anne Fine
18	*Dirty Beasts*	Roald Dahl
18	*Beethoven*	Robert Tine
18	*Mossflower*	Brian Jacques

17	*Mort*	Terry Pratchett
17	*Honey I Shrunk/Blew Up the Kids*	
17	*Goggle-Eyes*	Anne Fine
16	*Better than Life*	Rob Grant and Doug Naylor
16	*The Story of Tracey Beaker*	Jacqueline Wilson
16	*Call Waiting*	R. L. Stine
16	*Everyone Else's Parents Said Yes*	Dea Heriditary
15	*Bravo Two Zero*	Andy McNabb
15	*Kristy Series*	Ann M. Martin
15	*Buddy*	Nigel Hinton
15	*The Vampire's Promise*	Caroline B. Cooney
15	*Dark Portal*	Robin Jarvis
15	*The Colour of Magic*	Terry Pratchett
15	*Heaven*	Virginia Andrews
14	*The Shining*	Stephen King
14	*Henry Sugar*	Roald Dahl
14	*Ramona*	Beverley Cleary
14	*White Fang*	Jack London
14	*Beauty and the Beast*	
14	*The Second World War*	
14	*Freckle Juice*	Judy Blume
14	*It's Not the End of the World*	Judy Blume
14	*The Phantom*	Christopher Pike
14	*13 Tales of Horror*	A. Finnis (ed.)
14	*Soccer at Sandford*	Rob Childs
14	*The Stranger*	Caroline B. Cooney
13	*There's an Awful Lot of Weirdos in Our Neighbourhood*	Colin McNaughton
13	*Stacey* series	Ann M. Martin
13	*Wuthering Heights*	Emily Bronte
13	*The Whitby Witches*	Robin Jarvis
13	*The Queen and I*	Sue Townsend
13	*The Playmate*	Herbert Richardson
13	*It's Not Fair*	Bel Mooney
13	*Jane Eyre*	Charlotte Bronte
13	*Animal Farm*	George Orwell
13	*Around the World in 80 Days*	Jules Vernes
13	*The Machine Gunners*	Robert Westall
13	*Martin's Mice*	Dick King-Smith
13	*The Pelican Brief*	John Grisham
13	*The Return of the Vampire*	Caroline B. Cooney
13	*The Mask*	Dean R. Koontz
13	*Bill's New Frock*	Anne Fine
13	*The Eighteenth Emergency*	Betsy Byars

13	*Frankenstein*	Mary Shelley
13	*Gremlins*	Angus MacVicar
13	*Free Willy*	Nigel Robinson
12	*Gulliver's Travels*	Jonathan Swift
12	*I Was a Teenage Worrier*	Ros Asquith
12	*Mrs Pepperpot* series	Alf Prøysen
12	*Iggie's House*	Judy Blume
12	*Harry's Mad*	Dick King-Smith
12	*The Haunted House*	Jan Pienkowski
12	*The Enchanted Wood*	Enid Blyton
12	*Great Expectations*	Charles Dickens
12	*The Call of the Wild*	Jack London
12	*The Crystal Maze*	Peter Arnold
12	*Summer Dreams, Winter Love*	Mary Francis Shura
12	*Carrie's War*	Nina Bawden
12	*Batman*	
12	*Salamanastron*	Brian Jacques
12	*Kidnapped*	Francine Pascal
11	*Star Wars*	George Lucas
11	*The Light Fantastic*	Terry Pratchett
11	*Jack and the Beanstalk*	
11	*My Secret Admirer*	Carol Ellis
11	*The Reaper Man*	Terry Pratchett
11	*The Bible*	
11	*To Kill a Mockingbird*	Harper Lee
11	*Uncanny*	Paul Jennings
11	*Carpet People*	Terry Pratchett
11	*Diggers*	Terry Pratchett
11	*Hitchhiker's Guide to the Galaxy*	Douglas Adams
11	*David Copperfield*	Charles Dickens
11	*The Magician's Nephew*	C. S. Lewis
11	*Manchester United*	
11	*One Nil*	Tony Bradman
11	*Pride and Prejudice*	Jane Austen
11	*The Snow Spider*	Jenny Nimmo
10	*Snow White*	
10	*The Owl who was Afraid of the Dark*	Jill Tomlinson
10	*Martin the Warrior*	Brian Jaccques
10	*Heard It in the Playground*	Allan Ahlberg
10	*The Horse and His Boy*	C. S. Lewis
10	*Hound of the Baskervilles*	Sir Arthur Conan Doyle
10	*How Dogs Really Work*	Alan Snow
10	*The Magic Faraway Tree*	Enid Blyton
10	*Funny stories*	

10	*Conrad's War*	Andrew Davies
10	*Rhyme Stew*	Roald Dahl
10	*The Little Mermaid*	Hans Christian Andersen
10	*The Little Princess*	Frances Hodgson Burnett
10	*Lords and Ladies*	Terry Pratchett
10	*Petals on the Wind*	Virginia Andrews
10	*In the Pool*	Jan Ormerod

The most obvious starting point in considering these lists is the extra-ordinary popularity of Roald Dahl's books. Eight of the ten favourite individual titles are by Dahl. Even more notable, perhaps, is the finding that ten of the top twenty favourites cited in List 1 are by Dahl, since in that list individual titles are being ranked alongside series of books which may include up to 200 individual titles. We discuss Roald Dahl's popularity later in this chapter.

Peter Benton, who conducted a survey of Year 8 (12-year-olds) reading which runs in parallel to our own work, raised interesting questions about how far the 'classics' are still read as part of pupils' leisure pursuits (Benton, 1995). Our findings suggest a fairly wide readership for certain 'classic' children's titles: *The Hobbit, The Secret Garden, The Lion, the Witch and the Wardrobe* and *Black Beauty* all appear in the top twenty most read titles. *Lord of the Rings, The Wind in the Willows, Little Women, Alice in Wonderland, The Railway Children, Oliver Twist, The Diary of Anne Frank, Heidi, Treasure Island* are all in the top 100 titles. *Winnie the Pooh, Jungle Book* and *Peter Pan* also appear.

Whilst the notion of a 'classic' is a debatable one which, we will argue later (in chapter 8), is not particularly helpful in advancing the discussion of the quality of the texts children are reading, the construct has a certain power. Clearly it represents a view of literary heritage which for some parents creates a powerfully nostalgic link with their own childhood experiences of reading. Children's classics are part of the currency of cultural capital which extends through adulthood. But the divisions between high and popular culture implicit in notions of the classics do not bear much investigation. It is highly likely that many of the children who reported reading *Winnie the Pooh, Jungle Book* and *Peter Pan* were reading the Disney versions. Many children were able to ascribe the names of the original authors to the texts, which might suggest that the originals were being read, but the evidence is inconclusive. Disney book versions of *Winnie the Pooh* might fall into Peter Benton's category of 'literary fast food', whereas it seems unlikely that the A. A. Milne version would be described in this way. Simplistic categorisation of classic and non-classic texts are generally less than helpful; a child who has enjoyed the Disney film and book versions of *Winnie the Pooh* might move on to read the original, or vice versa. Certainly, the reason for the prominence of *The*

Secret Garden and *Little Women* in the data we gathered seemed very likely to be related to the film versions of the stories which were on general release just prior to the time of the survey.

Nevertheless, it is interesting to note that traditional classics do appear in the lists of favourite titles. If we consider the 100 most popular titles other children's and adult classic titles appear: *White Fang, Wuthering Heights, Jane Eyre, Animal Farm, Around the World in Eighty Days, Gulliver's Travels, Great Expectations, Kidnapped, To Kill a Mockingbird, David Copperfield, The Magician's Nephew, Pride and Prejudice, The Horse and His Boy, The Hound of the Baskervilles*. One in six titles in our top 200 then might be considered 'children's classics' and this does not take into account titles which many might consider 'modern classics' such as *The Borrowers, The Iron Man, Watership Down, Charlotte's Web, Stig of the Dump* and *The Silver Sword*.

The importance of media influence on children's reading choices is obvious. Of the titles in the top 100 the following, at least, had enjoyed a high media profile (usually either a cinema or television adaptation) in the five years prior to the survey: *The BFG, The Witches, Jurassic Park, The Secret Garden, The Lion, the Witch and the Wardrobe, Madam Doubtfire, Winnie the Pooh, Watership Down, Aladdin, Jungle Book, Robin Hood, Take That, Dracula* and *Little Women*. In the next most popular one hundred titles a number of other books appear which are clearly linked to media productions: *The Wizard of Oz, The Mask, Beethoven, Honey I Shrunk/Blew Up the Kids, The Shining, Beauty and the Beast, The Pelican Brief, Frankenstein, Gremlins, Free Willy, The Crystal Maze, Batman, Star Wars, Hitchhiker's Guide to the Galaxy, Manchester United, The Little Mermaid*. Therefore approximately one in every seven books in our list had some sort of media tie-in. However the analysis of answers to the question 'Do you have a favourite writer or favourite series of books?' offers another perspective on this finding, since media influence is less strong when respondents note their favourite author or series (rather than recording their actual reading in the previous month).

A range of genres is represented in the top thirty book titles. Of our genre categories (described in the previous chapter), six appear in these thirty most-often-mentioned books. 'Adventure' is by far the most popular genre followed by 'Romance/Relationships and Growing Up', then 'Horror' and 'Science fiction/Fantasy', then 'Comedy' and then 'Animal-Related Fiction'. The absence of non-fiction in the top 100 titles is notable, with only *The Diary of Anne Frank* and *Take That*, having more than twenty mentions.

Favourite series

What then are the most popular series? Some children mentioned the name of a series rather than an individual title, as explained above. List 3, which follows, gives the number of times particular series were mentioned by name. It should be read in conjunction with the list of individual titles, since it is notable that books in some series are often mentioned by title rather than by series name. This is particularly true of the *Point Horror* series which is very widely read. Twenty-eight *Point Horror* titles appear in the top 100 books mentioned.

List 3: most frequently mentioned series

199	*The Famous Five*	Enid Blyton
160	*Adrian Mole*	Sue Townsend
139	*Babysitter I, II & III*	R. L. Stine
91	*The Secret Seven*	Enid Blyton
80	*Babysitters Club*	Ann M. Martin
75	*Garfield*	Jim Davis
74	*Asterix*	Rene Goscinny
69	*Sweet Valley High/Twins/University*	Francine Pascal
66	*Red Dwarf*	Grant Naylor
62	*The Beano*	
47	*The Saddle Club*	Bonnie Bryant
46	*What Katy Did*	Susan Coolidge
44	*Anastasia*	Lois Lowry
41	*Worst Witch*	Jill Murphy
38	*Point Horror*	
36	*Mr Majeika*	Humphrey Carpenter
30	*Goosebumps*	R. L. Stine
29	*The Dandy*	
29	*Naughtiest Girl*	Enid Blyton
26	*Home Alone I & II*	
26	*Sherlock Holmes*	Sir Arthur Conan Doyle
25	*Jessica*	Francine Pascal
25	*Sonic*	
25	*Ghost stories*	
25	*Redwall*	Brian Jacques
23	*Monty*	Colin West
22	*It shouldn't Happen to a Vet*	James Herriot
22	*Vlad the Drac*	Ann Jungman
21	*Napper*	Martin Waddell
20	*Jill's Riding Club*	Ruby Ferguson
20	*Biggles*	W. E. Johns
20	*Dennis the Menace*	
20	*Hardy Boys*	Franklin W. Dixon
20	*Tintin*	Hergé
19	*Puzzle Adventure/Island*	J. Tyler/G. Waters
19	*My Girl and My Girl II*	Patricia Hermes

19	*Freshman*	Lynda A. Cooney
19	*Sharpe's Company/Eagle*	Bernard Cornwell
19	*Dilly the Dinosaur*	Tony Bradman
19	*Computer books*	
18	*Shoot*	
18	*Poems*	
18	*Mallory Towers*	Enid Blyton
18	*Where's Wally?*	Martin Handford
17	*Paddington*	Michael Bond
17	*Honey I Shrunk/Blew Up the Kids*	
16	*Mr Bean*	R. Driscoll
15	*Kristy*	Ann M. Martin
13	*Stacey*	Ann M. Martin
12	*Mrs Pepperpot*	Alf Prøysen
11	*Star Wars*	George Lucas
11	*Agent Arthur*	Usborne Publishing

The book lists related to age and sex

The lists above give an indication of the most popular individual titles for the whole sample. They do not indicate which books are most popular with boys or girls, or with children at different ages. We thought it important to divide our information in this way, and so the following lists give information on most popular individual titles and series for each age group and sex. The highly gendered nature of children's reading choices is discussed more fully in Chapter 4 of this book.

As explained previously, it is sometimes difficult to separate individual titles from series and in these lists individual titles within a series have been amalgamated under the series name. For instance *Asterix in Spain*, *Asterix the Gaul* and other such titles are listed simply as *Asterix*. Individual titles in such series as *Point Horror* and *Babysitters Club* are amalgamated similarly.

Lists 4, 5 and 6 detail boys' favourite titles and series at the three ages we investigated. There are 71 titles on the list of 10-year-old boys' favourites. What does it tell us? Certainly that Roald Dahl is, unsurprisingly, highly popular; and that Enid Blyton is also popular with this group. Clearly, 10-year-old boys enjoy adventure and humour. These genres dominate the list. There is too a strong interest in books about football. Several of the favourite books would probably be considered 'classics': *Oliver Twist, Gulliver's Travels, Peter Pan, The Wind in the Willows, Black Beauty, The Secret Garden, The Hobbit* and *The Lion, the Witch and the Wardrobe* all appear in the list. Only one poetry book appears, *Revolting Rhymes*, by Roald Dahl. The commonly held assumption that boys of this age are more interested in non-fiction than narrative is not supported by these findings. Only two non-fiction books, *The Guinness Book of Records* and dinosaur books (presumed various), appear on the list.

The fact that there is a shorter list for 12-year-old boys than for 10-year-old boys is, in part, an indication of the wider reading in the older age group – there is a long list of books with five or fewer mentions. Twelve-year-old boys are reading slightly less than 10-year-olds, and fewer of these boys are reading the same texts. Roald Dahl, perhaps because of the irreverent nature of some of his stories, is still popular at this age, but Enid Blyton is losing her appeal. The interest in war and science fiction stories which can be observed amongst 10-year-old boys becomes more noticeable at 12, as does an increased interest in fantasy and horror stories. Again, non-fiction does not feature prominently; only *The Guinness Book of Records* is mentioned by more than five respondents in this category. What is not obvious from List 5, but is clear from the total list of titles read by 12-year-old boys is the number of books, mentioned by one or two children only perhaps, which might be considered adult reading. Among these are books by Agatha Christie, Stephen King, Terry Pratchett, Tom Clancy, Ian Livingstone, John le Carré, and Alistair Maclean.

Amongst 14-year-old boys, the trend towards more eclectic reading continues. Fourteen-year-olds read a wider range of books than younger boys and fewer read the same texts. Roald Dahl is still remarkably widely read by 14-year-olds, but his work is now nearly matched in popularity by Stephen King's. Four Stephen King books appear in List 6 but a number of others, for example, *Dolores Claiborne*, *The Tommy Knockers*, *The Dark Half*, were also mentioned by boys of this age. The *Point Horror* series appears to have become too tame, and boys of this age have moved onto fiercer material, whilst at the same time retaining an affection for Roald Dahl, an author they know from their younger days. *Asterix* retains his appeal which spreads across age groups. The huge popularity of *Jurassic Park* might be accounted for by the fact that the film of the book appeared at about the time of the survey, although a number of other Michael Crichton books appear on the full list, for example, *Congo* (four mentions) and *Rising Sun* (two mentions). Terry Pratchett is also very widely read, but the size of his *œuvre* means that no one title appears in this list. He did in fact receive 49 mentions as ascribed author, compared to 86 for Roald Dahl and 68 for Stephen King, the two other most popular authors for 14-year-old boys as judged by books listed.

List 4: favourite titles and series amongst 10-year-old boys

20+ mentions

62	*The Twits*	Roald Dahl
61	*The Famous Five* series	Enid Blyton

55	*Fantastic Mr Fox*	Roald Dahl
48	*Charlie and the Chocolate Factory*	Roald Dahl
46	*The BFG*	Roald Dahl
44	*Matilda*	Roald Dahl
42	*James and the Giant Peach*	Roald Dahl
36	*The Magic Finger*	Roald Dahl
31	*Jurassic Park*	Michael Crichton
31	*George's Marvellous Medicine*	Roald Dahl
29	*The Secret Seven* series	Enid Blyton
28	Ghost stories	Presumed various
26	*The Witches*	Roald Dahl
22	*The Turbulent Term of Tyke Tyler*	Gene Kemp
21	*Garfield* series	Jim Davis
20	*Goosebumps* series	R. L. Stine
20	*Charlie and the Great Glass Elevator*	Roald Dahl
20	*Danny the Champion of the World*	Roald Dahl
20	*Asterix* series	Rene Goscinny

10–19 mentions

19	*The Hobbit*	J. R. R. Tolkien
17	*Sonic The Hedgehog* series	Martin Adams
16	*Napper* series	Martin Waddell
15	*The Animals of Farthing Wood*	Colin Dann
15	*Dilly the Dinosaur* series	Tony Bradman
14	*Mr Majeika* series	Humphrey Carpenter
14	*Tintin*	Hergé
13	*The Secret Garden*	Frances Hodgson Burnett
13	Dinosaur book	Presumed various
13	*The Iron Man*	Ted Hughes
12	*Boy*	Roald Dahl
12	*The Wind in the Willows*	Kenneth Grahame
12	*Treasure Island*	R. L. Stevenson
11	*Home Alone I & II*	A. L. Singer/Todd Strasser
11	*The Big Match* series	Rob Childs
10	*Peter Pan*	J. M. Barrie
10	*Red Dwarf* series	Grant Naylor
10	*Revolting Rhymes*	Roald Dahl
10	*Stig of the Dump*	Clive King
10	*Soccer at Sandford*	Rob Childs
10	*Dennis the Menace* series	
10	*Aladdin*	
10	*Esio Trot*	Roald Dahl

5+ mentions

9	*Oliver Twist*	Charles Dickens
9	*Playmate*	Herbert Richardson
9	*How Dogs Really Work*	Alan Snow
9	*Superfudge*	Judy Blume
9	*Alien*	Jane O'Brien
8	*One Nil*	Tony Bradman
8	*Where's Wally?* series	Martin Handford
8	*Vlad the Drac*	Ann Jungman
8	*Truckers*	Terry Pratchett
8	*The Mask*	Dean R. Koontz
7	*Black Beauty*	Anna Sewell
7	*Gulliver's Travels*	Jonathan Swift
7	*True Monster Stories*	Terry Deary
7	*Flat Stanley* series	Jeff Brown
7	*The Guinness Book of Records*	
7	*Mr Bean* series	R. Driscoll
7	*Mrs Doubtfire*	Anne Fine
7	*Jungle Book*	Rudyard Kipling
7	*The Worst Witch* series	Jill Murphy
7	*Monty* series	West Colin
6	*Hardy Boys* series	Franklin W. Dixon
6	*Going Solo*	Roald Dahl
6	*Gremlins* series	Angus McVicar
6	*Woof*	Allan Ahlberg
6	*Winnie the Pooh*	A. A. Milne
6	*Conrad's War*	Andrew Davies
6	*Redwall* series	Brian Jacques
6	*The Lion, the Witch and the Wardrobe*	C. S. Lewis
6	*Iron Woman*	Ted Hughes

List 5: favourite titles and series amongst 12-year-old boys

20+ mentions

52	*The BFG*	Roald Dahl
42	*The Witches*	Roald Dahl
41	*Charlie and the Chocolate Factory*	Roald Dahl
35	*Point Horror* series	
38	*Adrian Mole* series	Sue Townsend
28	*Asterix* series	Rene Goscinny
27	*Jurassic Park*	Michael Crichton
27	*The Twits*	Roald Dahl

26	*Matilda*	Roald Dahl
24	*The Hobbit*	J. R. R. Tolkien
23	*The Red Dwarf* series	Grant Naylor

10–20 mentions

19	*James and the Giant Peach*	Roald Dahl
19	*George's Marvellous Medicine*	Roald Dahl
17	*Boy*	Roald Dahl
14	*Fantastic Mr Fox*	Roald Dahl
13	*Garfield* series	Jim Davis
12	*Biggles* series	W. E. Johns
11	*It*	Stephen King
11	*The Lion, the Witch and the Wardrobe*	C. S. Lewis

5+ mentions

9	*The Guinness Book of Records*	
9	*The Secret Seven* series	Enid Blyton
8	*Mort*	Terry Pratchett
7	*Buddy*	Nigel Hinton
7	*The Famous Five* series	Enid Blyton
7	*Revolting Rhymes*	Roald Dahl
7	*The Magic Finger*	Roald Dahl
7	*Danny the Champion of the World*	Roald Dahl
6	*Sonic the Hedgehog*	Martin Adams
6	*Superfudge*	Judy Blume
6	*United* series	Michael Hardcastle
6	*Mossflower*	Brian Jacques
6	*Freeway Fighter*	Ian Livingstone
6	*Martin the Warrior*	Brian Jacques
6	*Esio Trot*	Roald Dahl
6	*Lord of The Rings*	J. R. R. Tolkien

List 6: favourite titles and series amongst 14-year-old boys

20+ mentions

40	*Jurassic Park*	Michael Crichton
23	*Red Dwarf* series	Grant Naylor
22	*Adrian Mole* series	Sue Townsend

10–19 mentions

19	*It*	Stephen King
17	*The Hobbit*	J. R. R. Tolkien
16	*Sharpe's (Rifles)* series	Bernard Cornwell
15	*Lord of the Rings*	J. R. R. Tolkien
15	*Asterix*	Rene Goscinny
13	*The BFG*	Roald Dahl
12	*Point Horror* series	
11	*Star Wars* series	George Lucas
11	*The Witches*	Roald Dahl
11	*The Twits*	Roald Dahl
11	*Pet Cemetery*	Stephen King

5+ mentions

9	*Bravo Two Zero*	Andy McNabb
9	*Charlie and the Chocolate Factory*	Roald Dahl
9	*Garfield*	Jim Davis
9	*James and the Giant Peach*	Roald Dahl
9	*Dracula*	Bram Stoker
8	*George's Marvellous Medicine*	Roald Dahl
8	*Boy*	Roald Dahl
7	*Better than Life*	Rob Grant and Doug Naylor
7	*Misery*	Stephen King
6	*Puzzle Island* series	J. Tyler/G. Waters
6	*Watership Down*	Richard Adams
6	*The Shining*	Stephen King
6	*Matilda*	Roald Dahl
6	*Danny the Champion of the World*	Roald Dahl
6	Encyclopedia	Various

Lists 7, 8 and 9 relate to 10-, 12- and 14-year-old girls' favourite titles. Sixty-one individual or series titles were mentioned more than five times by our sample of 10-year-old girls. Clearly, Roald Dahl is as popular with girls of this age as he is with boys. Seven of the fifteen most popular titles are written by him, but the most popular Dahl book for 10-year-old boys, *The Twits*, does not figure here at all. There is a notable tendency for girls of this age to read series. There are 20 series mentioned here, more than in any of the lists for boys. Obvious too is an interest in animals, particularly horses, and animal stories. It seems too that the obvious preference of older girls for fiction centred on romance, relationships and growing up is being established at this age, as evidenced by the popularity of the *Babysitter* and *Sweet Valley* series, and the presence of titles such as *Little*

Women, Oliver Twist, My Girl, The Secret Garden, Are You There God? It's Me Margaret, and the *Adrian Mole* series.

Twelve-year-old girls' enjoyment of series reading is also clear from list 8, but one series, *Point Horror*, is overwhelmingly the most popular reading for girls of this age. Roald Dahl retains a high level of popularity but is much less popular with 12-year-old than 10-year-old girls. The interest in reading about animals and horses starts to wane, but the interest in relationships and romance is clear. Indeed, books in the *Point Horror* series, though plotted around horrific events, often have themes centred on relationships and growing up, which may explain why boys are less interested in this series. The list does not give any indication that girls of this age often read 'adult' fiction. This is in contrast to the reading habits of boys at the same age; a significant proportion of boys appear to establish adult reading preferences before girls do. Since boys' reading declines from 12 to 14, this finding does not necessarily imply that this earlier move to read fiction marketed for an adult readership is helpful to boys' reading development. Rather, it seems to us to imply that girls are more able than boys to find reading material which matches their interests and concerns and has been written for a teenage market.

As with boys, there is a trend for girls to read an increasing range of books as they get older. Amongst 14-year-old girls fewer of the same individual titles are read by large numbers of girls. However the popularity of series reading, particularly the *Point Horror* series, with girls complicates the picture. It would seem that there are two trends. In general girls read an increasing range of books as they get older. Those books that are read by a large number of girls mainly occur in series. Increasingly, as they get older, girls are reading the same series.

What else can be said about the books that 14-year-old girls read? Romance, relationships, growing up and horror figure large as themes in the books in List 8 and in increasingly sophisticated forms, for example, *To Kill a Mockingbird, Wuthering Heights, Jane Eyre, Little Women, Silence of the Lambs, Pet Cemetery, It, Forever, Dracula, Misery*. What is indicated by this list, and confirmed by the longer list of all books read by girls of this age is the popularity of 'adult' fiction. As with boys of this age, girls are enjoying books, particularly those by Virginia Andrews, that might be enjoyed by their parents.

List 7: favourite titles and series amongst 10-year-old girls

20+ mentions

73	*Matilda*	Roald Dahl
68	*The Famous Five* series	Enid Blyton
66	*The Babysitters Club* series	Ann M. Martin

61	*Sweet Valley* series	Francine Pascal
57	*The BFG*	Roald Dahl
44	*Charlie and the Chocolate Factory*	Roald Dahl
40	*Fantastic Mr Fox*	Roald Dahl
39	*I Can't/It's Not Fair* series	Bel Mooney
39	*Point Horror* series	
37	*The Secret Garden*	Frances Hodgson Burnett
36	*The Magic Finger*	Roald Dahl
36	*Black Beauty*	Anna Sewell
33	*James and the Giant Peach*	Roald Dahl
28	*The Secret Seven* series	Enid Blyton
23	*George's Marvellous Medicine*	Roald Dahl
23	*Goosebumps* series	R. L. Stine
20	*Anastasia* series	Lois Lowry

10–19 mentions

19	*Alice in Wonderland*	Lewis Carroll
19	*Little Women*	Louisa May Alcott
19	*Nancy Drew* series	Carolyn Keene
18	Ghost story	Presumed various
18	*My Naughty Little Sister* series	Dorothy Edwards
16	*Mr Majeika* series	Humphrey Carpenter
15	*Please Mrs Butler*	Allan Ahlberg
14	*Room 13*	Robert Swindells
13	Horse and pony stories	Presumed various
12	*Flat Stanley*	Jeff Brown
11	*Superfudge*	Judy Blume
11	*Beauty and the Beast*	
11	*The Animals of Farthing Wood*	Colin Dann
11	*Garfield* series	Jim Davis
11	*Bill's New Frock*	Anne Fine
10	*Aladdin*	
10	*Harry the Dirty Dog* series	Gene Zion
10	*Esio Trot*	Roald Dahl

5+ mentions

9	*Heidi*	Johanna Spyri
9	*Revolting Rhymes*	Roald Dahl
9	*Dirty Beasts*	Roald Dahl
9	*Paddington* series	Michael Bond
9	*Charlotte's Web*	E. B. White
8	*Jill's Pony* series	Ruby Ferguson

8	*Johnny Briggs* series	Joan Eadington
8	*Sophie* series	Dick King-Smith
8	*Take That*	
8	*But You Promised*	Bel Mooney
7	*Puzzle Island* series	J. Tyler/G. Waters
7	*My Girl*	Patricia Hermes
7	*Cinderella*	
7	*Beethoven I & II*	Robert Tine
7	*Charlie and the Great Glass Elevator*	Roald Dahl
7	*Boy*	Roald Dahl
6	*Snow White*	
6	*Oliver Twist*	Charles Dickens
6	*Mrs Pepperpot* series	Alf Prøysen
6	*Brenda the Bold*	Jean Ure
6	*Are You There God, It's Me Margaret*	Judy Blume
6	Fairytales	
6	*Flossie Teacake* series	Hunter Davis
6	*Flour Babies*	Anne Fine
6	*Fudge-a-Mania*	Judy Blume
6	*Adrian Mole* series	Sue Townsend

List 8: favourite titles and series amongst 12-year-old girls

20+ mentions

358	*Point Horror* series	
127	*Sweet Valley* series	Francine Pascal
67	*Babysitters Club* series	Ann M. Martin
58	*Matilda*	Roald Dahl
38	*The Witches*	Roald Dahl
36	*BFG*	Roald Dahl
34	*The Twits*	Roald Dahl
30	*Charlie and the Chocolate Factory*	Roald Dahl
30	*Adrian Mole*	Sue Townsend
23	*What Katy Did* series	Susan Coolidge
20	*George's Marvellous Medicine*	Roald Dahl

10–19 mentions

19	*The Secret Garden*	Frances Hodgson Burnett
18	*Forever*	Judy Blume
17	*James and the Giant Peach*	Roald Dahl
17	*Boy*	Roald Dahl
15	*Tiger Eyes*	Judy Blume

15	*The Hobbit*	J. R. R. Tolkien
15	*Danny the Champion of the World*	Roald Dahl
14	*Anastasia* series	Lois Lowry
13	*Saddle Club* series	Bonnie Bryant
13	*Superfudge*	Judy Blume
12	*The Diary of Anne Frank*	Anne Frank
10	*Deenie*	Judy Blume
10	*Fantastic Mr Fox*	Roald Dahl
10	*Dracula*	Bram Stoker
10	*Just as Long as We're Together*	Judy Blume

5+ mentions

9	*My Girl*	Patricia Hermes
9	*Nancy Drew* series	Carolyn Keene
9	*Are You There God, It's Me Margaret*	Judy Blume
8	*The Lion, the Witch, and the Wardrobe*	C. S. Lewis
8	*Esio Trot*	Roald Dahl
8	*Garfield*	Jim Davis
8	*Goggle-Eyes*	Anne Fine
7	*The Famous Five* series	Enid Blyton
7	*The Worst Witch*	Jill Murphy
7	*Blubber*	Judy Blume
7	*It's Not the End of the World*	Bel Mooney
7	*The Borrowers*	Mary Norton
7	*Charlotte's Web*	E. B. White
6	*Not Dressed Like that You Don't*	Yvonne Coppard
6	*The Secret Seven* series	Enid Blyton
6	*Back Home*	Michelle Magorian
6	*Winnie the Pooh*	A. A. Milne
6	*Then Again, Maybe I Won't*	Judy Blume
6	*Tales of a Fourth Grade Nothing*	Judy Blume
6	*Goodnight Mr Tom*	Michelle Magorian
6	*Henry Sugar*	Roald Dahl
6	*Home Alone I & II*	A. L. Singer/T. Strasser
6	*I Was a Teenage Worrier*	Ros Asquith
6	*Jurassic Park*	Michael Crichton
6	*Little Women*	Louisa May Alcott
6	*Black Beauty*	Anna Sewell

List 9: favourite titles and series amongst 14-year-old-girls

20+ mentions

365	*Point Horror* series	
26	*Flowers in the Attic*	Virginia Andrews
25	*Adrian Mole* series	Sue Townsend
23	*Forever*	Judy Blume
22	*It*	Stephen King
20	*Babysitters Club* series	Ann M. Martin

10–19 mentions

17	*The Witches*	Roald Dahl
15	*The BFG*	Roald Dahl
14	*Matilda*	Roald Dahl
11	*Misery*	Stephen King
11	*Charlie and the Chocolate Factory*	Roald Dahl
11	*Sweet Valley* series	Francine Pascal
10	*The Firm*	John Grisham
10	*Jane Eyre*	Charlotte Brontë

5+ mentions

9	*Silence of the Lambs*	Thomas Harris
9	*Little Women*	Louisa May Alcott
9	*Pet Cemetery*	Stephen King
9	*Heaven*	Virginia Andrews
9	*Jurassic Park*	Michael Crichton
8	*Are You There God, It's Me Margaret*	Judy Blume
8	*Petals on the Wind*	Virginia Andrews
8	*The Saddle Club* series	Bonnie Bryant
8	*Dracula*	Bram Stoker
8	*Boy*	Roald Dahl
8	*The Client*	John Grisham
8	*Jill's (Pony)* series	Ruby Ferguson
7	*The Lion, the Witch and the Wardrobe*	C. S. Lewis
7	*Goodnight Mr Tom*	Michelle Magorian
7	*The Twits*	Roald Dahl
7	*Wuthering Heights*	Emily Brontë
6	*The Secret Garden*	Frances Hodgson Burnett
6	*To Kill a Mocking Bird*	Harper Lee
6	*My Sweet Audrina*	Virginia Andrews
6	*The Rats*	James Herbert

| 6 | *Garfield* series | Jim Davis |
| 6 | *The Famous Five* series | Enid Blyton |

Favourite authors and series

Children were asked whether they had a favourite writer or series of books. Of the 7,976 respondents, 5,169 (64.8 per cent) did name a favourite. Listed below are all the authors or series mentioned ten times or more.

List 10: favourite authors and series

Author/series	Number	As % of sample
Roald Dahl	1,834	22.99
The *Point Horror* series	595	7.45
Enid Blyton	498	6.24
Judy Blume	217	2.72
Stephen King	208	2.60
Francine Pascal/*Sweet Valley High*	162	2.03
Terry Pratchett	116	1.45
Dick King-Smith	112	1.40
Ann Martin/*The Babysitters Club*	87	1.09
Steve Jackson/Ian Livingstone/ *Fighting Fantasy* series	82	1.02
Virginia Andrews	76	0.95
R. L. Stine	75	0.94
J. R. R. Tolkien	61	0.76
Sue Townsend	58	0.72
C. S. Lewis	53	0.66
Christopher Pike	53	0.66
Brian Jacques	50	0.62
Colin Dann/*Farthing Wood*	50	0.62
Grant Naylor/*Red Dwarf*	40	0.50
Franklin Dixon/*The Hardy Boys*	40	0.50
Bonnie Bryant/*The Saddle Club*	38	0.47
Carolyn Keene/*Nancy Drew* series	32	0.40
Robin Jarvis/*Deptford Histories*	32	0.40
Puzzle Adventures	29	0.36
Charles Dickens	28	0.35
Agatha Christie	27	0.33
Michael Hardcastle	27	0.33
Douglas Adams/*Hitchhiker's Guide*	27	0.33
Paula Danziger	24	0.30

Author/series	Number	As % of sample
Point Romance	24	0.30
James Herbert	23	0.28
Danielle Steel	23	0.28
Asterix	21	0.26
Willard Price	21	0.26
Robert Westall	20	0.25
Catherine Cookson	19	0.23
Anne Fine	19	0.23
James Herriott	19	0.23
Jim Davies	16	0.20
A. A. Milne / *Winnie the Pooh*	14	0.17
Arthur Ransome	13	0.16
Beatrix Potter	13	0.16
Adventure books	13	0.16
Goosebumps	12	0.15
Jennings books	11	0.13
Michael Crichton	11	0.13
Beano books	11	0.13
Disney books	10	0.12
David Eddings	10	0.12
The Borrowers books	10	0.12
Bel Mooney	10	0.12

Clearly there are correspondences between this list and the book list of the titles which had been most widely read in the four weeks prior to the survey. Again, we have placed individual authors alongside series of books, and this inevitably leads to overlaps (for example, for authors who write for different series) and some inconsistencies in the numbers (for example, we attributed Winnie the Pooh to A. A. Milne, but the Disney books category might have been intended). Nevertheless, the outstanding popularity of Roald Dahl is clear – he has over three times as many mentions as the next most popular writer mentioned. Some 'classic' writers for children and adults are named: C. S. Lewis, J. R. R. Tolkien, Arthur Ransome, A. A. Milne, Beatrix Potter and Charles Dickens. Several very popular writers of 'adult' fiction are mentioned: Stephen King, Virginia Andrews, Agatha Christie, James Herbert, Danielle Steele, Catherine Cookson, James Herriott and Michael Crichton.

In 1994, 64.8 per cent of respondents were able to name a favourite writer or series, whereas only 49.9 per cent of the sample responded to this question in Whitehead's 1971 survey. In our view this is likely to be attributable to the attention to authors in schools and in the marketing of

Table 2.1 Favourite authors, 1971 and 1994

Author	Number of children naming as favourite author, 1971	Number of children naming as favourite author, 1994	1994 top 30 position
Enid Blyton	1,604	498	2
Charles Dickens	158	28	23
Agatha Christie	121	27	24
R. L. Stevenson	120	3	—
W. E. Johns	96	4	—
Alistair Maclean	57	8	—
Ian Fleming	56	2	—
C. S. Lewis	54	53	13
H. G. Wells	51	3	—
A. Conan Doyle	45	9	—
Anthony Buckeridge	43	0	—
Louisa M. Alcott	43	0	—
Jules Verne	41	0	—

books. Author visits and readings, letters to authors, the drawing of pupils' attention to an author's body of work – all of these are regular features of school life which serve to promote children's awareness of authorship. Whitehead lists the 1971 pupils' top 13 authors in his report. They make an interesting comparison and are therefore listed in Table 2.1. Where children in the 1994 survey named the same author as a favourite, the numbers are given in the final column.

C. S. Lewis maintains a remarkably consistent place over the two decades. Otherwise the change since 1971 in the balance between male and female writers is noticeable, as is the increasing influence of the media on the 1994 choices.

The top ten favourite authors

We can investigate further the characteristics of the different groups of children who name particular favourite authors. The data show, for example, that higher percentages of socio-economic groups C_2, followed by D/E and C_1, named Roald Dahl as their favourite author than groups A and B. More boys than girls (24 per cent : 21 per cent) chose Dahl as their favourite, and the percentages naming him as a favourite declined in the teenage years (30 per cent of 10-year-olds; 26 per cent of 12-year-olds and 12 per cent of 14-year-olds). Nevertheless, Dahl maintains an un-challenged lead in terms of overall popularity. This is discussed further in the Endpiece to this chapter.

Point Horror is named as a favourite by far more girls than boys, and by a higher percentage of social group A than any other group. As one might expect, the *Point Horror* series becomes more popular amongst older children – there is a leap in the series' popularity from 10- to 12-year-old girls which is sustained and increased at 14.

For Enid Blyton readers that age trend is reversed. Roughly double the number of girls to boys name her as their favourite writer, and her popularity increases as one moves down the social scale. Judy Blume is more likely to be named as a favourite in social group A, although generally her appeal seems to be consistent across socio-economic groups. The choice is clearly gender related – she is more popular with girls – and the largest percentage naming her as a favourite falls in the 12-year-old age range. Stephen King becomes more popular with older children and a higher percentage of boys than girls across all social groups. Francine Pascal's following is largest in group C_1 amongst girls, aged 12 particularly. Terry Pratchett is most popular amongst boys of 12 and 14, with a higher percentage readership in social groups B and A.

Dick King-Smith is named fairly evenly by both sexes as their favourite author, with higher percentages from the youngest of our age groups and in socio-economic group A. The *Babysitters Club* and *Fighting Fantasy* series are highly gender related, to girls and boys respectively, but across all social groups. Both of these series are most popular amongst 12-year-olds.

Favourite authors 10–30

Of the next twenty most often named favourite authors, some of the writers were chosen by a markedly higher percentage of girls than boys. These were Virginia Andrews, R. L. Stine (the *Point Horror* series), Christopher Pike (another *Point Horror* author), Bonnie Bryant (the *Saddle Club* series) and Agatha Christie. Three authors were named only by girls: Carolyn Keene (the *Nancy Drew* series), Paula Danziger and Danielle Steele. The only author to be named a favourite solely by boys was Michael Hardcastle (who writes football stories), although Brian Jacques, J. R. R. Tolkien, Grant Naylor (the *Red Dwarf* series), Douglas Adams and Franklin Dixon (the *Hardy Boys* series) were named predominantly by boys. It is interesting to note which authors were more or less equally named by both sexes: Sue Townsend, C. S. Lewis, Robin Jarvis, Charles Dickens and James Herbert.

In terms of age, only C. S. Lewis, Michael Hardcastle, Robin Jarvis and Carolyn Keene were named roughly equally across the three age groups. Colin Dann, Bonnie Bryant and Charles Dickens were most often specified as favourite authors in the 10-year-old group. R. L. Stine, Paula Danziger and Brian Jacques were mostly named by 12-year-olds, and Sue Townsend, Franklin Dixon and Douglas Adams by 12- and 14-year-olds.

The writers that were named mainly by 14-year-olds were Virginia Andrews, J. R. R. Tolkien, Christopher Pike, Grant Naylor, James Herbert, Danielle Steele and Agatha Christie.

The data relating socio-economic group and favourite authors are not generally noteworthy at this lower end of the 'top 30' list, but certain points seem worthy of comment. Sue Townsend, J. R. R. Tolkien, Robin Jarvis and Douglas Adams have a higher percentage of mentions in groups A and B. Christopher Pike has the highest percentage in group D/E, as does Charles Dickens, who is not named as favourite amongst the A group. The numbers of mentions are, however, small when this part of the list is divided into socio-economic groups.

When considered in relation to ethnicity, the findings about favourite authors coincide with those in most other parts of the questionnaire – i.e. few significant differences emerge between the reading choices of one broad group and another. However, the percentage of 'white' children naming *Point Horror* as a favourite series was double the percentage of those in other groups. Books by Judy Blume and those in the *Sweet Valley High* series attract an ethnically more diverse readership than other named favourites. The *Saddle Club* series and James Herbert were mentioned only by children who identified themselves as 'white'.

We end with summary Tables 2.2–2.6 which show the patterns by age and sex of those children who named the top five writers/series as their favourites, i.e. Roald Dahl, *Point Horror*, Enid Blyton, Judy Blume and Stephen King.

Table 2.2 Boys and girls naming Roald Dahl as favourite author by age

Age	% boys within age group	% girls within age group
10+	30.6	29.7
12+	27.6	24.2
14+	13.5	10.6

Table 2.3 Boys and girls naming *Point Horror* as favourite series by age

Age	% boys within age group	% girls within age group
10+	2.2	4.5
12+	3.0	14.3
14+	2.0	16.2

Table 2.4 Boys and girls naming Enid Blyton as favourite author by age

Age	% boys within age group	% girls within age group
10+	6.4	15.0
12+	3.7	7.2
14+	1.5	2.0

Table 2.5 Boys and girls naming Judy Blume as favourite author by age

Age	% boys within age group	% girls within age group
10+	0.5	2.7
12+	0.5	7.7
14+	0.4	5.4

Table 2.6 Boys and girls naming Stephen King as favourite author by age

Age	% boys within age group	% girls within age group
10+	0.9	0.0
12+	2.7	1.8
14+	6.1	4.8

Summary

- Roald Dahl's books are extraordinarily popular. Eight of the ten favourite individual titles recorded in the *Children's Reading Choices* survey are by Dahl.
- There is a fairly wide readership for certain 'classic' children's titles. The popularity of classic texts is often linked to film and television adaptations, and it is not clear how many children are reading original, rather than, for example, Disney versions of the text.
- One in seven of the books read in the month before the survey had an obvious media tie-in.
- Adventure is the most popular genre of children's fiction.
- Very little non-fiction features in the top 100 titles.
- Children are enthusiastic about reading books that are organised into series, which carry with them a degree of familiarity.

- Ten-year-old boys enjoy adventure, humour and books about football. Ten-year-old girls enjoy reading books about animals, romance, relationships and growing up. The commonly held assumption that boys of this age are more interested in non-fiction than narrative is not supported by these findings.
- Twelve-year-old boys and girls read a wider range of texts than 10-year-olds. Boys of this age are more likely than girls to read fiction marketed for adult readers. Twelve-year-old boys enjoy war and science fiction stories, fantasy and horror. Again, non- fiction does not feature prominently. Twelve-year-old girls enjoy books about relationships and romance.
- Fourteen-year-old boys and girls have more eclectic reading tastes than 10- or 12-year-olds. At 14, many girls and boys are reading 'adult' fiction which might be enjoyed by their parents.
- In general girls read an increasing range of books as they get older. Those books that are read by a large number of girls mainly occur in series. Increasingly, as they get older, girls are reading the same series. Fourteen-year-old girls enjoy reading books about romance, relationships, growing up and horror. Fourteen-year-old boys enjoy science fiction, fantasy and horror.
- About 65 per cent of respondents to the *Children's Reading Choices* survey could identify a favourite author or series, compared to about 50 per cent of respondents in 1971. C. S. Lewis has maintained a consistent degree of popularity over the two decades. Otherwise the changes between 1971 and 1994 occur in the balance between male and female writers and the increasing influence of the media.

Endpiece: Roald Dahl and Enid Blyton

The *Children's Reading Choices* survey reveals the outstanding popularity of Roald Dahl. Our findings about favourite books, and about Dahl in particular, are supported by other surveys. In a 1995 survey by the School's Curriculum and Assessment Authority, Dahl was the most frequently read author for 8- and 11-year-olds in school (SCAA, 1995). Millard's 1994 survey suggested that although on the whole boys and girls choose different titles and different authors, the boys' and girls' lists converge at the level of the most popular children's authors, that is in the books of Dahl and Blyton (Millard, 1997). This is a phenomenon also noticed by Bardsley (Bardsley, 1991). In a poll organised by the BBC *Bookworm* programme and Waterstones, the booksellers, in 1997, more than 10,000 people who voted decided that when it comes to entertaining children, Dahl was the master. *The Times* proclaimed 'Britain's favourite children's book is Roald Dahl's *Matilda*' (*The Times* 1.9.97). There were three lists in the BBC poll: the top twenty books enjoyed by under-sixteens, the adult choice of the best children's book, and the overall positions. All readers irrespective of age decided that *Matilda*, the story of a book-loving child who exacts revenge on her parents when they force her to watch television instead, was their favourite. In the children's list in the BBC/Waterstones poll Dahl's books took seven of the top ten places, almost exactly the same findings as in the *Children's Reading Choices* survey.

In our survey, Dahl has over three times as many mentions as the next most popular individually named writer, who is Enid Blyton. Blyton herself, it is claimed, is the best-selling English language writer of the twentieth century, the author of approximately 700 books for children. In 1951 alone she wrote 37 books. In the last year of her life when she was suffering from serious illness she wrote four. Blyton died in 1968, but still sells a staggering number of books each year world wide – 8 million annually according to the *Observer* newspaper (7.9.97); 6 million in 1995 according to Cullingford (1998).

Blyton, of course, is now subject to much criticism. If Dahl is considered by some to be outrageously entertaining, Blyton has been called 'the author of the world's most boring dialogues' in books which are 'as comforting as Instant Whip' (*The Times* 1.9.97) written in a vocabulary so limited that it is 'drained of all difficulty until it achieve(s) a kind of aesthetic amnesia' (quoted in Carpenter and Pritchard, 1995). Critics have labelled her plots predictable, her characters two dimensional and her style repetitive. Nevertheless Blyton maintains an enormous following. Children in our survey nominated the *Famous Five* books as the most popular series, outscoring by quite some way more modern writing such as the *Adrian Mole* books, *The Babysitters Club*, or the *Sweet Valley High* series. And Blyton's *Secret Seven* series is the fourth most popular book series.

Certainly, then, these are writers to whom we should pay special attention, if only because of their popularity. Margaret Meek emphasises the importance of these widely read stories: 'Any significant theory of children's literature cannot ignore the texts children hold in common, for on those is their view of literature founded, and from those are their competencies developed' (Meek, 1980). What is it about Dahl and Blyton that appeals so strongly to children? Something in these books 'connects' with children, making large numbers want to read them and individuals want to read large numbers of them. What is there in the Blyton and Dahl books that 'connects'?

At first glance they are very different authors. Dahl's tales often have a dark and subversive side to them. Carpenter and Pritchard note that 'Dahl's stories seem objectionable to many adult readers, who find them a mixture of the glutinous and the cruel' (Carpenter and Pritchard, 1995). *The Witches* was placed on the 'restricted list' in San Diego schools after some parents complained that it frightened their children or encouraged them to take an interest in the occult. Roald Dahl features more prominently than any other author in the list of the fifty books which were most frequently challenged in schools and public libraries in the United States between 1990 and 1992: *The Witches* stands at number nine in the list, *Revolting Rhymes* at number fifteen and *James and the Giant Peach* at number thirty. Dahl's books certainly contain heinous crimes, such as the poisoning of a bad-tempered grandmother with toilet cleaner (*George's Marvellous Medicine*), and the killing of two grumpy aunts in *James and the Giant Peach*:

> Aunt Spiker immediately tripped over Aunt Sponge and came down on top of her. They both lay on the ground, fighting and clawing and yelling and struggling frantically to get up again, but before they could do this, the mighty peach was upon them.
>
> There was a crunch.
>
> And then there was silence.
>
> The peach rolled on and behind it, Aunt Sponge and Aunt Spiker lay ironed out upon the grass as flat and thin and lifeless as a couple of paper dolls cut out of a picture book.
>
> (Dahl, 1967)

Blyton would never confront her readers with such events. Her characters, and their pets, live in a world where there are clear moral codes of conduct and behaviour. Hers is a safe old-fashioned world, though it has been suggested that to the modern eye, Quentin's rages and George's precarious gender identification in the *Famous Five* series raise questions for psychoanalytic approaches to literary criticism. Serious objections to the stereotypical and discriminatory views expressed in Blyton's books are well documented in, for example, Sheila Ray's (1982) and Bob Dixon's (1974, 1977) work. Cullingford quotes the example of Sniffer's father, a traveller ('What a nasty piece of work he is! Why doesn't he get a hair cut?') who is described as being 'more like an odour than something living' (Cullingford, 1998).

Dahl's outlook is also disturbing. He is reported to have declared: 'Parents and schoolteachers are the enemy. The adult is the enemy of the child because of the awful process of civilising this thing that is an animal with no manners, no moral sense at all' (*The Sunday Times* 5.7.95). There are sadistic elements in his books, cruel dénouements (the hero of *The Witches* ends up as a mouse), and violence. Giants in *The BFG* eat children 'like popcorn' and when in dispute engage in the most terrifying violence 'they punched and kicked and scratched and bit and butted each other as hard as they could . . . blood flowed. Noses went crunch, teeth fell out like hailstones'. His characters use rude words and make rude noises. There is a darkness and energetic pessimism in Dahl's bizarre stories; Sarland even talks of Dahl's 'incipient fascism' (Sarland, 1983). The stories are brightened by humour and, often, a wittiness in the plot, but there is usually a feeling that evil is lurking just around the corner.

Blyton, on the other hand, is comforting. Her readers enjoy the security of a domestic world where the adults are conventional, predictable and in charge, but not often present. Like many classic children's stories, such as the C. S. Lewis *Narnia* series, *Peter Pan* and *Swallows and Amazons* in which groups of children organise themselves without adult intrusion, Blyton takes the young reader on an escapist adventure. The seductiveness of this element in her stories is illustrated by the memories of the poet Brian Patten:

> Blyton helped me to escape from a drab room in a drab house. She smuggled me down through secret depths to underwater doors that baffled and delighted me . . . hidden tunnels, lost passageways, the whole lichen-coated paraphernalia of forbidden places . . . She transported me beyond the reaches of school time and bedtime and the thou-shalt-not grown up world.
>
> (*Sunday Times* 12.1.97)

Blyton offers children an enticing invitation. She offers them the chance to behave with independence in the world she creates, to be members of a special small club which makes its own decisions, and with that group to take part in an exciting adventure.

There are though a number of elements in the writing of both authors which are common and which help to explain their popularity. Both write in unfussy prose. In both the plot moves at a fast pace, with few descriptive longueurs, and regular climactic moments en route to the plot's major denouement. The character types are easy to identify and express their characteristics in largely unequivocal behaviours, appearances and actions. In books by both authors, the text is presented in manageable chunks, and the narrative voice is close to the child's situation, in the sense that the narrator's persona often seems to be almost a bedtime story-teller, a friendly adult in close contact with the child reader. There is a good deal of dialogue in the novels, which generally simplifies the demands made upon the child's reading skills, and enhances the dialogic, open qualities of the texts. For an immature reader there is little danger of getting lost or confused in a Dahl or Blyton book. Both writers can quickly capture attention. A reader does not have to spend time 'getting into' the book. *Danny the Champion of the World* begins: 'When I was four months old, my mother died suddenly and my father was left to look after me all by himself' (Dahl, 1975).

Perhaps even more important than these narrative techniques is the fact that both authors provide readers with an exciting child-centred world. The stories of Blyton (for example, the *Mallory Towers* books) and Dahl (for example, *James and the Giant Peach, Matilda, Danny the Champion of the World*) often reflect the universal predicament of the child learning to survive without his or her parents. Children in these books are allowed a considerable measure of independence. They are given the freedom to go off and have their own adventures free from adult interference; children do good in a world where adults are often badly behaved. In the worlds which Blyton and Dahl create children are resourceful and daring. Here their readers can safely indulge their fears and fantasies of life without adult control.

Perhaps this deliberate exclusion of adult culture is the reason why both authors raise such antipathy in some adults. The novels are written to appeal predominantly to children, and not the overseeing adult – in this they contrast, for example, with the way that A. A. Milne appeals to the adult reader's sense of irony throughout the *Winnie the Pooh* series. Dahl in particular takes the side of children against adults. There is, almost, a rebellious two-fingered gesture to the adult world in some of his books (for example, in Matilda punishing her father and humiliating her headteacher, or Danny ruining Mr Victor Hazell's shooting party, or the child-substitute foxes getting the better of Farmers Bunce and Bean). But Blyton too is on children's side, especially because she takes their play so seriously. Many children love the books of Blyton and Dahl but both writers have in various places and at various times had their work banned by adults. It might be argued that Dahl and Blyton appeal to children exactly because they share a genuine child-centredness to which many, or most, adults no longer have access (in the same way that teenage girls' magazines have a format and a register directed at particular age group which deny or, at least, impede adult access). Ensuring that the childhood culture of the books is in some ways closed to adults is bound to appeal to children. How many adults will fall into fits of giggles in the way children do at some of the language in the Dahl books – snozzcumbers, bottoms, and boiled slobbages?

There are of course other factors which give Dahl and Blyton the lead in popularity. Both are backed by formidably successful marketing. Indeed there is a commercial company whose business is solely devoted to the commercial exploitation of Blyton's works and characters. Both authors have had their work translated into other media, which, as is obvious from other titles in our lists, gives rise to increased popularity. Blyton's stories are in comics, and on television, and her characters feature on everything from cereal bowls to bed linen. A number of Dahl's books have been adapted into cinema versions by Hollywood.

There is too the fact that both write books which fall into the adventure category, the genre which is clearly the favourite for these age groups (as we have discussed already). The fact that adventure is by far the most popular genre amongst readers of this age is confirmed by other contemporary studies (*Contemporary Juvenile Reading Habits*, 1994, British National Bibliography Research Fund Report 69). Appleyard suggests that the appeal of adventure fiction for young readers lies in the combination of 'sameness and diversity' that is common to the genre: 'What to adults seems repetitive in these stories must to the child appear confirmation that in diverse new areas of experience, what counts is still recognisable and familiar' (Appleyard, 1990). The appeal, then, might be said to lie in the balance of familiarity with a limited amount of newness, security with just a frisson of danger.

Both Enid Blyton and Roald Dahl were prolific writers. Dahl, of course, published less than Blyton, who is said to have habitually written between 6,000 and 10,000 words a day, and in the late 1940s produced more than thirty books a year (Stoney, 1974). But twelve of Dahl's novels came into our top fifty titles. Children know they can trust these authors for entertainment and hence revisit them for the certainty of more of the same. Familiarity is a motivating force. Gabrielle Cliff Hodges points out that as children move from picture books to more demanding texts 'the inclination is to travel in the company of reliable friends' (Cliff Hodges, 1996). A well-loved author can become a comfort blanket; the certainty of more of the same is highly reassuring and enjoyable. This does not, of course, apply solely to immature readers, as the popularity of such popular adult fiction as the Inspector Wexford and the Morse detective novels illustrates. Dahl and Blyton benefit from the same phenomenon which makes the *Point Horror* and *Sweet Valley High* books so popular: they provide a clearly signposted route to enjoyment. The reader 'enter(s) into a fellowship of readers with whom you can share your pleasure and enjoyment' (Cliff Hodges, 1996) so a virtuous circle of popularity is created; the popularity of an author creates further popularity through the fact that the reading of that author becomes an explicit social practice, rather in the same way that viewers watch television soap operas which become part of their own social world.

Blyton's and Dahl's contributions to the canon of high quality children's literature will no doubt continue to be debated, but their ability to lure literally millions of children into reading means that their huge contribution to children's literacy can hardly be disputed. One clear message emerges for those who would want to encourage children's reading: the way to get children reading is not to lecture them but to entertain them.

References

Appleyard, A. (1990) *'Becoming a reader': the Experience of Fiction from Childhood to Adulthood*, Cambridge: Cambridge University Press

Bardsley, P. (1991) *Factors Relating to the Different Reading Attitudes, Habits and Interests of Adolescents*, Research Affiliateship Report no. 1 New Zealand Dept. of Education, Massey University

Benton, P. (1995) 'Recipe fictions: literary fast food? Reading interests in Y8' *Oxford Review of Education*, 21, pp. 108–11

Carpenter, H. and Pritchard, M. (1995) *The Oxford Companion to Children's Literature*, Oxford: Oxford University Press (5th reprint)

Cliff Hodges, G. (1996) 'Encountering the Different' in Styles, M., Bearne, E. and Watson, V. *Voices Off*, London: Cassell

Contemporary Juvenile Reading Habits, 1994, British National Bibliography Research Fund Report 69

Cullingford, C. (1998) *Children's Literature and its Effects*, London: Cassell

Dahl, R. (1967) *James and the Giant Peach*, London: George Allen and Unwin

Dixon, B. (1974) 'The tiny world of Enid Blyton' *Children's Literature in Education* no. 15, pp. 43–61

Dixon, B. (1977) *Catching Them Young: Sex, Race and Class in Children's Fiction*, London: Pluto

Fry, D. (1985) *Children Talk about Books: Seeing Themselves as Readers*, Milton Keynes: Open University Press

Meek, M. (1980) 'Prolegomena for a study of children's literature' in Benton, M. (ed.) *Approaches to Research in Children's Literature*, University of Southampton

Millard, E. (1997) *Differently Literate*, London: Falmer Press

Ray, S. (1982) *The Blyton Phenomenon: the Controversy Surrounding the World's Most Successful Children's Writer*, London: Deutsch

Sarland, C. (1983) 'The Secret Seven or The Twits: cultural clash or cosy combination? *Signal*, vol. 42, pp. 155–71

SCAA (1995) *One Week in March: a Survey of the Literature Pupils Read*, 1995, SCAA Discussion Paper no. 4

Stoney, B. (1974) *Enid Blyton: a Biography*, London: Hodder and Stoughton

Chapter 3

Periodical reading

In this chapter, we report the *Children's Reading Choices* survey findings on periodical reading in relation to magazines, comics and newspapers. We list the most popular titles and discuss the appeal of this reading to children of different ages and to both sexes. We discuss changes in periodical reading over time, and draw upon interview data to illustrate the importance and influence of periodicals in young people's reading. In the Endpiece, we discuss attitudes to teenage magazines and offer an analysis of one edition of the most popular teenage magazine.

Periodical reading

We were aware that a survey that sought information on children's voluntary reading ought not to confine itself solely to questions to do with books. As part of the *Children's Reading Choices* survey children were, therefore, asked about comics, magazines and newspapers they read regularly, an area of children's reading which adults do not always take seriously.

It is clear from responses to those questions that newspapers, comics (we define these as periodicals which consist wholly or mainly of stories told by means of picture strips), and magazines are widely read by children in all three of the age categories we investigated. One child in the sample listed eleven periodicals that were regularly read. Over a quarter (26.9 per cent) of the children in the sample regularly read five or more periodicals, 16 per cent read six or more periodicals regularly and 67 per cent read between one and five regularly. The main findings relating to the number of periodicals read are summarised in Table 3.1.

The survey allows some comparisons to be made between periodical reading and book reading. The overwhelming majority of the sample of 7,976 children – 83 per cent – reported regular reading of periodicals; this is a slightly larger percentage than those 79 per cent who said they had read a book in the four weeks prior to the survey. Whilst the figures

Table 3.1 Number of periodicals read regularly as percentage of total sample

No.	0	1	2	3	4	5	6	7	8	9	10
%	18	5.9	15.0	18.5	16.2	11.3	6.7	3.6	2.3	1.2	1.7

cannot be directly compared, they are indicative of the amount of reading taking place, and they are supported by findings related to purchase of reading material.

Responses to the survey question asking children to tell us whether they had bought a book, a comic, a magazine, or a newspaper 'this year' suggest that in relation to the total sample the most commonly purchased item was a magazine, followed by a book, a newspaper, and then a comic (Table 3.2). It is clear from the figures that girls are more likely to buy books and magazines than boys, whereas boys are more likely to buy comics and newspapers than girls. The pattern of book buying is remarkably similar in each age group, but this is not the case with newspapers, comics and magazines. The purchase of comics decreases as children grow older, whilst the purchase of newspapers and magazines increases with age. (Purchasing habits are discussed in greater detail in Chapter 6.)

In one question, children were asked their views on the amount of reading they did ('a large amount', 'quite a lot', 'about an average amount', 'not very much', or 'only a little') (Table 3.3). We considered the relationship between responses to this question and the information about whether the children were reading magazines, comics or newspapers. It is notable that even amongst children who see themselves as reading 'only a little' two-thirds of the sample read periodicals. The percentage figures for periodical reading amongst the first three categories – prolific to average readers – are very similar.

Table 3.2 Purchase of books, magazines, comics and newspapers over the year by age

No. of items	10+	12+	14+
1 book	35.9	32.6	31.8
2+ books	12.1	13.3	14.1
1 comic	34.2	24.5	1.6
2+ comics	6.0	5.2	2.8
1 magazine	51.3	54.4	51.1
2+ magazine	19.9	32.3	39.1
1 newspaper	27.5	35.2	38.1
2+ newspapers	4.6	7.7	8.1

Table 3.3 Association between reported amount of reading and periodical reading

	% of category who regularly read a periodical
Read a large amount	87.1
Read quite a lot	87.6
Read an about average amount	86.3
Read not very much	76.7
Read only a little	66.4

In summary, then, there is a good deal of periodical reading going on, a considerable amount of money is being spent on this type of reading material and children appear to want to look at a range of different periodicals, particularly as they grow older. Overall periodical reading increases with age from 10 to 14 years. There is heavier periodical reading by girls, but boys read more comics and newspapers than girls.

Favourite periodicals

What exactly is this reading material? What are the most popular periodicals for children within this age range? Fashions in individual titles are sometimes fairly fleeting, but the spread of titles is indicative of general patterns. Table 3.4 lists those periodicals read by more than 2 per cent of the sample.

We can fill out the picture provided by this list by considering each of the most popular periodicals in terms of the sex, age and social class of the readers. The important figures are contained in Table 3.5.

Various points of interest can be noted from these findings. It appears, for instance, that football magazines aimed at boys (*Match*, *Shoot*, *Manchester United*) are read by approximately equal numbers of boys in the different age categories, and across socio-economic groups. There is a slight fall in the percentage of 14-year-old boys reading *Match* and *Shoot*, but the interest is sustained (and probably transferred to other titles). There is a steady growth in newspaper reading relative to the child's age, and a more even balance between male and female readers for local and Sunday newspapers. The daily tabloid newspapers are notably more attractive to boys, in part, probably, because of the sports coverage.

Girls' magazines, on the other hand, have readerships drawn from particular age categories and, in general, from different socio-economic groups (*Big*, *Shout*, *Mizz*, *More*). Teenage girls' magazines are by far the most widely read periodicals in our survey. What struck us as most significant in this table was the dominant place of one particular title – *Just 17* – in girls' reading at the time of the survey. Nearly one in two girls in

Table 3.4 Most popular periodicals

Name	% of sample	Brief description
Just 17	21.5	girls' teenage magazine
Big	18.2	girls' teenage magazine
Smash Hits	16.2	teenage music magazine
The Sun	16.1	national tabloid newspaper
The Beano	13.0	children's comic
Match	10.1	boys' football magazine
Shoot	9.5	boys' football magazine
Shout	9.0	teenage music magazine
The Daily Mirror	8.3	national tabloid newspaper
Mizz	8.3	girls' teenage magazine
Fast Forward	7.7	teenage music/media
Newspaper	7.1	unspecified titles
The Dandy	6.6	children's comic
Computer magazines	5.7	unspecified titles
TV Hits	5.6	TV/media magazine
The News of the World	4.3	national tabloid Sunday newspaper
More	3.9	girls' teenage magazine
Live & Kicking	3.4	TV/music magazine
The Evening Post	3.3	local daily newspaper
Horse and Pony	3.0	special interest magazine
Football magazines	2.7	unspecified titles
Sega Power	2.1	computer games magazine
Manchester United	2.1	club football magazine

our sample regularly read this periodical. If that figure is broken down into age categories the place of this magazine in the reading diet of teenage girls becomes even more obvious (Table 3.6).

It is noticeable too that for many boys an interest in reading about football is a unifying factor across the age categories. Whitehead's 1971 survey showed a pattern of 10- and 12-year-old boys reading comics and moving on, at 14, to a more 'adult' interest in the football magazines. Now, over two decades later, boys at all three ages share a reading diet of sometimes rather dense statistical and biographical information about football and footballers, league tables and transfer fees.

Changes in periodical reading over two decades

How do patterns of children's periodical reading compare with the situation two decades ago? In some respects, children's appetite for this kind of reading material does not seem to have changed. Whitehead reports that there was 'extensive reading of comics and magazines by the majority of children throughout the age range' (p. 54). In 1971, the average number of periodicals read per child was 3.1; in 1994, it was 3.26.

Table 3.5 Most popular periodicals by age, sex and social group

Name	% boys	% girls	10+	12+	14+	Significant no. of readers by social group
Just 17	1.4	42.5	5.4	25.4	37.0	no sig. diff.
Big	2.1	35.0	13.9	22.9	19.0	C_1, C_2, D/E
Smash Hits	2.1	31.1	11.8	19.6	18.5	C_1, C_2, D/E
The Sun	17.7	14.2	12.1	17.9	18.8	C_1, C_2, D/E
The Beano	19.4	6.2	22.2	12.1	2.9	no sig. diff.
Match	18.1	1.5	11.1	10.6	8.0	no sig. diff.
Shoot	17.0	1.5	9.9	10.0	8.3	no sig. diff.
Shout	0.8	17.7	6.7	13.4	7.8	no sig. diff.
The Daily Mirror	9.0	7.6	6.0	8.7	10.6	C_1, C_2, D/E
Mizz	0.4	16.7	0.4	5.8	20.2	A, B
Fast Forward	1.7	14.0	11.1	8.2	3.2	C_1, C_2
'Newspaper'	8.1	5.9	4.3	8.2	9.3	A, B
The Dandy	10.4	2.6	11.8	5.7	1.2	no sig. diff.
'Computer magazines'	10.8	0.4	2.1	6.8	9.0	A, B, C_1
TV Hits	0.8	10.8	4.3	5.9	7.1	C_1, C_2, D/E
The News of the World	4.3	4.2	2.7	4.5	5.8	C_2, D
More	0.2	7.7	0.2	1.9	10.2	A, B
Live & Kicking	0.6	6.3	4.0	4.4	1.8	C_2, D/E
The Evening Post	3.6	3.2	1.3	3.1	6.1	C_1, C_2, D/E
Horse & Pony	0.2	5.9	4.4	3.0	1.4	C_1
'Football magazines'	4.9	0.4	3.3	2.8	1.8	C_1, C_2, D/E
Sega Power	2.6	0.1	1.1	1.8	1.2	no sig. diff.
Manchester United	2.8	1.3	2.0	2.3	1.9	no sig. diff.

Whitehead notes that 'at all ages girls read more periodicals than boys' (p. 54), and this remains true in the 1990s. However, Whitehead also noted 'a small but consistent decline in the amount of periodical reading with increasing age, particularly in the case of the boys' (p. 55). That trend is now reversed. It is clear from our findings that periodical reading increases with age from 10 to 14 years. Magazine and newspaper reading increases dramatically between 10 and 14, and only comic reading decreases. Girls, especially, read markedly more periodicals as they get older. Tables 3.7 and 3.8 set out this information.

In the 1971 survey girls were reading *Woman and Woman's Own*, women's magazines which Whitehead notes were 'probably bought for their mothers' (p. 154). *Jackie*, a teenage girls' magazine, had a wide readership of 12-year-olds (25 per cent of the age group) and an 'astonishing predominance' amongst 14-year-old girls, 'being read regularly by no fewer than 58 per cent of girls' (Whitehead p. 158). The trend, then, for one teenage girls' magazine to hold sway amongst the older girls has remained and been strengthened in recent years.

Table 3.6 Percentage of girls reading Just 17 within each age group

	10+	12+	14+
% girl readers of Just 17	10.7	51.4	68.8

Table 3.7 Number of periodicals read regularly, 1994 and 1971

Age	1994	1971
10+	2.62	3.29
12+	3.47	3.07
14+	3.78	2.91

Table 3.8 Number of periodicals read regularly by sex, 1994 and 1971

Age	Boys, 1994	Boys, 1971	Girls, 1994	Girls, 1971
10+	2.55	3.13	2.69	3.52
12+	3.18	2.93	3.79	3.25
14+	3.34	2.68	4.13	3.18
Mean	3.01	2.92	3.52	3.33

These historical comparisons confirm for us that periodical reading is today, and has been for many years, a very important element in children's reading diet. Trends are somewhat different, and those differences are worth noting for those who are interested in children's reading patterns and development. It is clear that large numbers of children are motivated to buy, swap and read magazines; for these reasons children's periodical reading needs to be taken seriously.

The appeal of periodical reading

In the interview phase of the *Children's Reading Choices* project many children spoke about the appeal of their magazines and comics. Certain themes emerged from what they said. Importantly, almost all of the children reported storing their magazines and returning to them for reference purposes, or simply for the pleasures of re-reading.

I keep all my magazines and if I've got nothing to do I take them out and just read them all again. (Girl, 12)

I go back to the interviews with people. Say you've read them, you sort of forget about them, so you go back to them, they don't really stick with you so . . . and I'd probably go back to new pop groups and stuff that might be coming out. Sometimes they put words in them, like *Smash Hits* you get word booklets and sometimes I go back to them to . . . say I wanted to learn the words of them. (Girl, 10)

All of the 14-year-old boys and all but one of the 14-year-old girls who read magazines reported that they returned to them. The boys re-read the 'funny bits', the news and scores; the girls go back to the problem pages, the beauty tips and stories and articles they particularly liked. Some reported this as a different kind of reading activity: 'getting down to serious reading' after 'skipping through' the first time round. Some used the magazines for reference purposes, particularly related to computer use:

Yes, in some of the computer magazines I've got, they tell you special moves. (Boy, 10)

In computer mags I get access codes and things. I've got a wicked cheat for my computer right, and you can go back into your mag and have a look at the cheat and it'll explain the game a bit more. (Boy, 10)

The re-reading often becomes a social act, shared with friends. Older boys talked about 'having a laugh' with the group reading of the magazines; a group of 14-year-old girls spoke about going back to articles that are 'good to talk about, like one on AIDS'. The initial reading seems for most to be a private one, in bedrooms or in front of the television; the re-reading is more likely to be shared.

If it's a computer mag, I usually go back to a cheat for a game but like, if it's a football mag I'm not very keen on football, but if one of my friends comes round, I'll just show him like a really good poster in it or something. (Boy, 10)

I read my comic out on the Estate. (Boy, 10)

If there's a bit I missed like in Gunz, I read them quite a few times, there's always bits that I've missed. A lot of information or whatever. I just use them for reference or to show people or whatever. (Boy, 14)

Another important theme threaded through the interviewees' comments concerned the way that magazines seemed to them to relate more closely to real life than books did.

Yes, I like books because . . . well I like magazines and it's real in magazines, but in books, it's not always real at all and it takes you away from the real world. And I also like reading books because I enjoy it. (Girl, 10)

There are interesting ambivalences in notions of the 'real world'. Sometimes reality is represented by information on the tastes, ages and preferences of celebrities or even fictional characters, and sometimes it is represented by the exploration of social problems or the grislier side of life. A 10-year-old girl, for example, thinking hard about this matter commented:

I don't really read non-fiction much, I don't find them as interesting. I know *Point Horror* are kind of non-fiction but they're different, they're more thrilling and more terrifying to me. (Girl, 10)

Others made the following points:

Mizz is alright, yeah. I like reading the true stories and the questions for the soap people, like *Home and Away* and that. (Girl, 10)

With *Smash Hits*, I like the way they tell you about the celebrities, my favourite pop group is Blur. They tell you all about their favourite things, their girlfriends, everything like that and what singles are coming out next. Who is getting married to who, new people who will be starring in new programmes. I just like the way they set it all out and they give you lots of posters to put on your wall and loads of stickers. (Girl, 10)

Bliss is full of teenage features, interesting stories, real life dramas, problem pages. It's a nice glossy magazine with good information about pop stars, the pop world and music, it's interesting. I like the problem pages and true life dramas and posters. (Girl, 14)

I think it's good [*Match*] because I like football as well. I've got it once or twice. It's usually more photos than anything else. It tells you about the teams, I like certain teams and the full league tables. I'd read it to see where my team is. (Girl, 12)

It's called *Games World*, it's got good information and it keeps me up to date really, it tells me what I can buy and what's good for me. Well, they do reviews on different games and give percentages and things and I like looking at that. (Boy, 14)

... the best bits are the reviews and the serious stuff about programming. (Boys, 14)

... I like to keep up to date with the latest news on players, transfers, and scores. I especially like the posters, the European articles and articles on my favourite club. (Boy, 14)

Problem pages and confessional articles are particularly popular with both boys and girls. There is a sense amongst many of the young people that these features offer opportunities to learn from the experience of others. They provide depersonalised opportunities for discussion of social, moral and ethical issues and encourage the readers to determine their own moral stance and possible courses of action in given sets of circumstances. One 12-year-old girl, for example, described how she covered the answers to problem page letters until she had decided upon her own view, and then enjoyed comparing her conclusions with the agony aunt's. Others described ways in which the articles gave them a chance to explore imaginatively some of the boundaries which constrained their own behaviours.

> I like the problem pages because you can read about other peoples' problems and if you've got like the same problems as them, you sort of get the same answer as them. (Girl, 10)

> I like reading this article, Mum Would Kill Me If She Knew. It would be like reading about things you're not supposed to do like smoking. I don't read the soap bits, it's boring because it just tells you what's happened already. (Girl, 10)

> I go back to the bits that girls shouldn't be doing. I don't know, because mostly the girls are getting into trouble and what they do is a bit silly and some of them do get out of problems mostly, yeah, they do get out of them. (Girl, 10)

The periodicals offer opportunities to fantasise, sometimes in the forbidden but appealing domains of violence:

> I like *Judge Dredd* because it's gory. I like the bits best where he's blowing them up, shooting people. My mate gets it for me, they're his and I just read them. (Boy, 10)

> Yeah, I read quite a few at home, I like Dennis The Menace, Batman Returns, Superman, that's it really. It tells you a lot, it tells you more about Batman and it shows you the characters, who they play with and in Superman, it's just like the same. I like the bits where they fight people, the baddies and things, the Joker and oh yes, the Riddler, he beats him up as well. (Boy, 10)

> I read some books but I prefer comics though. I like to go into a different world, just to forget everything. (Girl, 12)

> I like the *Beano*, the bits like where he's getting into trouble, like where he's doing silly things as well. (Boy, 10)

On the whole, the interviewees showed a strong sense of the relative benefits of one another's periodical reading.

> If we got caught reading this, that's it, our rep would go, but things like this aren't read because people have this hard image which is what us males are supposed to have. I hate to admit it but I'd read some advice pages, it's the image again, you can't say you read the female advice page, I mean, that's it, you'd get laughed out of school, you'd never be seen again . . . but some of it is quite useful. (Boy, 14)

> Boys, I think would like it [*Match*]. Boys like football and that. When they see *Match*, well, they like it. I'd like the Did You Know bits and the bits about TV. I'd read the good headlines, the crosswords, games. The poster of Man United. I wouldn't read the middle bit, all the scores, facts . . . it looks too boring. (Girl, 12)

Even one of the sterner critics accepts the case for plurality:

> I can imagine why boys like this, all this duffing up people, knocking things out, all this getting into trouble, but it's not really my kind of thing. I just like more down to earth things, stuff like that. They like, or boys like all this action thing. Some boys don't. There's a boy in our class called Richard, he likes classical music and he wouldn't ever listen to anything by Blur and he reads all these like classical novels and he doesn't read anything up to date and he wears old fashioned clothes and stuff. We don't take any notice because everyone has their own fashion in our class. (Girl, 10)

Many interviewees felt that they were influenced by the combination of the tone, style, content and editorial line of the various magazines.

> It's a very good magazine [*Just 17*]: good features, they're interesting and they keep you up to date in the latest fashions, freebies and things. It also tells you like in this article here about only having sex when you want to, and it tells you not to smoke and everything. They don't work all the time but they do have a certain influence on you when they describe the dangers and that does often change your mind. (Girl, 14)

> I like the way they talk in the magazine and the way they cover things like personalities and certain people. It's a very friendly magazine. (Girl, 14)

> I like the way it talks about players and that, it shows us about their social life, as well as being on the pitch. It also gives you an overall

view of what's happening in football. I like the beginning, the funny captions of players on the pitch and sometimes it interviews players and the players tell you what it was like on the pitch. It influences you to want to achieve the same goal, they tell you their feelings and emotions. (Boy, 14)

I suppose reading magazines like this is also good for boys to understand how girls feel and that, and what they go through in growing. (Boy, 14)

Just parts that I enjoy reading, like say I'm a bit of a Jürgen Klinsmann fan, sort of thing, and I just go back to his parts, parts of what he likes and cos he's my idol sort of thing, I want to know, like his favourite song, will probably be my favourite song. (Boy, 14)

In all of this the children's sense of periodical reading as an interactive experience is very clearly articulated. The magazines spark off a range of different activities including discussion, shopping, acting on beauty and make-up tips, swapping, changing opinions, using computers, and watching television, as well as individual and group reading. The relatively low status of the magazines and comics as cultural objects makes them user-friendly and adaptable in ways which allow them to fulfil decorative functions and be integrated into other texts. Children see the periodical reading process as provisional and different to book reading. They read in a non-linear manner in ways which sometimes approximate more to reading screens than to traditional ways of reading books.

... magazines are more interesting really than books. Sometimes I read horror books, they're a bit lively but that's it. In a book, you can't cut out pictures, in a magazine you can. (Girl, 10)

I find it [The Beano] quite fun. I read about half of it. I read Dennis and the bit in the middle. I don't read the last bit, Ivy The Terrible and the adverts. But this part in the middle, where you have to send away, I do look at that. In the middle there are things that you can send away for. I collect Dennis The Menace cards and things like a T-shirt, I've just sent away for that, I should get that tomorrow. It's got Dennis The Menace, it says it up at the top and I might get a Dennis The Menace hat. (Boy, 10)

Summary

- Newspapers, comics and magazines are widely read by children in all three of the age categories investigated. Over a quarter of the children in the sample regularly read five or more periodicals.

- Across the sample as a whole, the most commonly purchased item was a magazine.
- Girls are more likely to buy books and magazines than boys; boys are more likely to buy comics and newspapers than girls.
- The purchase of comics decreases as children grow older, whilst the purchase of newspapers and magazines increases with age.
- Two-thirds of the children who see themselves as reading 'only a little' do read periodicals.
- Football magazines aimed at boys are read by approximately equal numbers of boys in the different age categories, and across socio-economic groups.
- There is a steady growth in newspaper reading relative to the child's age.
- The daily tabloid newspapers are notably more attractive to boys, but there is a balance between male and female readers for local and Sunday newspapers.
- Girls' magazines tend to have readerships drawn from particular age categories and, in general, from different socio-economic groups.
- Teenage girls' magazines are by far the most widely read periodicals in the *Children's Reading Choices* survey.
- One particular title (*Just 17*) dominated girls' magazine reading.
- The trend for girls to read more periodicals than boys has remained since the 1970s; the 1970s trend towards a small but consistent decline in the amount of periodical reading with age is now reversed.
- Children report storing and re-reading their magazines, and returning to them for reference purposes.
- The ways in which magazines can be read (i.e. not cover-to-cover) appear to be part of their appeal.
- Problem pages and confessional articles are particularly popular with both boys and girls.
- Children report that they are influenced by what they read in periodicals.

Endpiece: teenage magazines

Teenage magazines, particularly those targeted at girls, are often poorly regarded by adults. In February 1996, for example, a Conservative member of the British Parliament introduced a Private Member's Bill which, if it had been passed, would have required teenage magazines to carry stickers indicating the age range for which they were suited. This was a response to a wave of outrage, fuelled by media coverage, about the explicit nature of some of the advice and information contained in various publications directed at teenage girls.

As Angela McRobbie (1997) has noted, opinion on this issue appeared to be quite strongly demarcated along gender lines. McRobbie's own developing analysis of the role of magazines in teenage girls' culture offers a particularly intelligent insight into the way the debates have been framed amongst radical cultural theorists since the 1970s, when *Jackie* held pride of place in young girls' affections (McRobbie, 1988; McRobbie and Nava, 1984. See also Barker, 1989; Walkerdine, 1987; Winship, 1987; and Radway, 1987). Nevertheless, faced with daughters or female pupils reading surprisingly explicit 'teenage' magazines, many adults feel a sense of discomfort and, sometimes, concern. It is these responses which we wish to consider here, particularly in relation to publications for girls – although boys' periodical reading is no less interesting. We have noted previously, for instance, that many boys share an interest in reading statistical and biographical information about football and footballers, and that this interest spans different ages. Boys' magazines often reflect the language and style of television football coverage, and, in doing so, reinforce a common vocabulary and set of conversational topics which can be heard amongst boys in playgrounds throughout Britain. This language and style is strongly gender related, but it is not, as in the past, particularly clearly demarcated by age. There has been a shortening of the period of childhood in the last two decades. Popular adult culture is now mediated and sold to younger children. The purchasing power of children of both sexes has increased, and for boys this means particularly the marketing of sport and its related products – sportswear, team souvenirs and the players themselves – to a younger audience. An induction for a 10-year-old boy into the football-related talk and reading of the secondary school would, therefore, offer him the language and knowledge to contribute to many adult conversations about football.

This is less obviously the case in the most popular teenage girls' periodicals, in which the language and topics are more clearly related to adolescence. In the 1995 magazines most widely read by girls in the survey, for example, boyfriends were designated 'boyfs' and swooning was not an uncommon response to excitement. The language does not provide an automatic entrée into the style of most adult women's talk. This, in itself, makes the girls' magazines more unsettling than the boys' to the adult reader.

It seems to us that there are three significant areas of adult doubt and worry about teenage girls' magazines. The first is connected with loss of innocence – a sense that children are prematurely catapulted into knowingness and concern about matters which would be better approached at a later stage. The second, which is enmeshed with the first, is a concern about values. How are children to negotiate their own moral paths through rampant consumerism? And through pressures to be sexually active from a young age? And through pressures to define their identities in potentially limiting terms (of appearance, fashion, relationships with the opposite sex, for example)? The third set of concerns we identify relate more directly to the reading process: the sense that reading magazines is a light and relatively trivial pursuit, and that it makes no contribution to reading development, either in terms of encouraging a worthwhile reading habit or of assisting the reader in becoming more skilled or discerning.

It seems to us that these tensions exist amongst teachers as well as parents. Teachers who are committed to positive initiatives to promote children's wider reading, and to validate children's reading choices are often uneasy about magazines. In the daily realities of the classroom, these tensions often emerge as unease about whether a teacher should permit a reluctant reader to read a magazine during a 'private reading' period, in which the reading material is apparently a matter of free choice.

These concerns turn on judgements of quality, of course. Questions about quality have become more complex and difficult to pose as the post-modernist enterprise has opened up thinking about the literary canon, and reader response approaches have encouraged an elasticity in thinking about what an individual reader might gain from a particular text. But however hedged around with difficulties, questions of quality do not, and should not recede in importance. Teachers have a responsibility to develop a child's reading, and they have legitimate agendas about the kinds of knowledge and values they wish to promote. In order to do this well, they need a view of the magazines which form an important part of children's leisure reading – a view which considers the content of the magazines, and the types of demands that content makes upon young readers in terms of strategies and approaches. This starting point acknowledges the child's interests and abilities and allows the teacher to exercise a professional responsibility to support the child's development.

The most useful starting point for a consideration of these questions, and a judgement about the validity of adult anxieties, seemed to us the magazines themselves. We therefore begin with a content analysis of an edition of *Just 17*, the most popular title in our survey, from April 1995.

What knowledge, information and values might a young reader have gleaned from this edition of *Just 17*? The cover advertises 'Pregnancy Scares: What You Should Know' and the magazine contains a good deal of information on sex and sexuality and procedures for young people who have emotional or physical problems relating to sex. The report on 'pregnancy scares' is set out very clearly with a large central photograph of a 16- or 17-year-old girl looking serious but confident. The article begins by running through the ways of becoming pregnant, offering definitions of more technical vocabulary ('ovulation', 'withdrawal method') in brackets. It deals with myths about notionally 'safe' times or places to have sex, including the idea that getting pregnant is impossible before menstruation begins. It explains how to get 'emergency contraception', and how to be tested for pregnancy, including where to go, any costs involved and the advantages and disadvantages of each option. The section titled 'If the Results are Positive' suggests who to talk to (parents first, although 'the idea of telling Mum and Dad might seem as appealing as a week-long maths exam'), and the options in terms of keeping the baby, adoption and fostering and abortion. The article ends with six highlighted contact addresses.

The final ten pages of the magazine are devoted to 'advice'. This takes various forms beginning with the 'advice report' on pregnancy scares and moving on to a double page spread of problem letters answered by a woman; a regular letter feature 'Don't call me weird but . . .'; problem page letters answered from 'a boy's view'; 'My Guilty Secret' a more developed confessional style of article followed by advice; a page of 'sex related problems' answered by a woman under the byline 'Confidential', an A–Z guide to sex and 'Celeb Therapy' a regular feature in which celebrities discuss problems they have faced and offer advice which is given editorial support. Three of the letters and the Celeb Therapy feature are written from a male perspective. A wide range of issues has been selected including: flirting, being pregnant at 13, being a 15-year-old attracted to a 35-year-old neighbour, depression, alcoholism, having a boring boyfriend, finding traditionally feminine pursuits (including being attracted to boys) unappealing, being homosexual, swearing, being too tall, being a virgin, not being a virgin, how to kiss people, being attracted to a step-brother, how to handle a violent attack, discharges, dating, masturbation and penis size. There are 17 different advice line telephone numbers on these pages, including 'The Condom Line', the Samaritans and the 'Coping with your first period' line. Four of the ten pages carry a tickertape-styled legend across the bottom of the page: 'remember: to be sussed is a must *but* sex under 16 is illegal'. There is very little over-printing on these pages, and the layout and fonts are more conventional and less provisional looking than elsewhere in the magazine. The images on these pages are predominantly face-to-camera portraits, usually of girls looking serious and wearing unremarkable clothes. Three of the advisers' photographs are featured; both Nick Fisher, who gives the 'boy's view' and Annabel G, the confidential adviser on sexual problems, have photographs which make them look rather older and more worldly than others featured on these pages.

The style is snappy with short sentences punctuated by exclamations and questions. Language levels move carefully between the 'scientific' and the vernacular, defining terms where there might seem to be the need and addressing the reader in a direct and informal manner. The sentence quoted above serves as an example: 'the idea of telling Mum and Dad might seem as appealing as a week-long maths exam'. The form 'telling Mum and Dad', as opposed to 'telling *your* Mum and Dad' is one that would only generally be used within a family, most often by siblings who shared the same parents. The inclusiveness of the construction, which places the writer alongside the reader, offers a form of subliminal reassurance. The following would serve as a further example of the care with which the article has been crafted:

> Plenty of foreplay – hugging, kissing, petting – beforehand helps to get you in the mood and encourages the vagina to produce a special lubricant. This makes it easier for your boyf's tackle (wearing a condom, of course!) to enter your vagina.

Foreplay is defined clearly. The passive voice of the first sentence maintains a distance for the generalisable scientific tone and vocabulary – *the* vagina, special *lubricant*. The personalised, vernacular use of 'your boyf's tackle' allows the writer to position herself, through the use of brackets and the exclamation mark, alongside the girl who would never dream of having sex without contraception, and then to distance herself from the serious and more formal formulation 'enter your vagina'. Again the writer of the article positions her/himself alongside the reader without being sententious or overly clinical. These carefully written lines offer information, formal and informal registers, language which will help the reader discuss her experiences, and a clear value statement about the need for contraception.

Other sources of information come from advertisements and advertising features. These give information on clothing and accessories, make up, sanitary protection, a newly released film, the *Sweet Valley High* series of romances, training opportunities, a bank, a charity for children, a new magazine and a radio station. Information features which do not advertise directly include brief reviews of films, videos and music, short 'fact files' on celebrities, a report on changes in school rules, a feature on relaxing when you feel stressed and a double page spread headed 'Dead Ugly' on unsightly looking animals which are threatened with extinction.

All of these features and advertisements offer the reader something to make up her mind about. She is being sold an image of herself as a consumer – discerning, interested in fashion, sex, music, films, books and animal welfare. The animal feature, for example, offers a 'campaigners' view' and a contact number for a conservation organisation, whilst presenting the information about the threatened species in the form of a set of beauty problems. The overarching guiding figure throughout the magazine as a whole is the reader as knowing consumer – relatively independent, though open to advice and in need of support and friendship.

The text presents certain sorts of reading demands. The variety of fonts, over-printing and use of colour create different levels of difficulty. Information is presented in chunks and gobbets, but where an editorial decision has been made about the need to synthesise, it is presented more systematically and in less provisional looking formats. The provisional nature of much of the presentation – as faxes, or notices on a board, or graffiti – combines with the dedication of a considerable proportion of space to readers' letters, poems and articles. These give the magazine an interactive dimension which offers encouragement to the reader to see herself as a writer. In Roland Barthes' (1977) terms *Just 17* is a 'readerly' text in that its codes are easily accessible to the reader, but is is also a 'writerly' text in the sense that considerable elements of it need to be 'written' by those who see themselves as readers. Within the act of reading the text is an invitation, both figurative and literal, to write.

There is plenty here upon which a teacher of reading/literature might build. The implied reader as knowing consumer might not be ideal, but she has certain qualities which might usefully be developed in her bodily counterpart. Not least of these is a sense of emerging independence and the right to make choices. She is used to a multi-media dimension to her texts and, in postmodern terms, to a destabilised open text. In her reading she is frequently called upon to empathise, to identify with people and animals, and sometimes to offer judgements. Stories are presented swiftly and succinctly, with an emphasis upon plot and accounts of emotion. The predominant literary form is a heightened realism which places consider-able emphasis on the apparent authenticity of experience. Information is given in abundance, clearly and accurately in an unpatronising manner often supported by artwork. There is an assumption that having read new information, the reader will need to talk it through to make sense of it.

Where does that leave us in relation to the three areas of adult doubt and worry about teenage girls' magazines which we identified earlier? Without doubt, these magazines work from an assumption of sexual knowingness which many adults might find uncomfortable to encounter. But an evening's television viewing – even before the 9 o'clock watershed – will leave most viewers in little doubt about the degree of knowledge and range of issues most young people confront on a daily basis. A little eavesdropping on young teenage girls' conversations will confirm their interest, their knowledge levels, and, generally, an underestimate of the sophistication of their understanding. In the light of this, nostalgia for a bygone era of innocence and ignorance seems fruitless.

The value position is explicitly that of an independent consumer, in need of support. Certainly, girls are encouraged to take style and appear-ance seriously; they are not encouraged to be subservient or undiscerning. They are encouraged to hold strong views, to enjoy themselves, to seek fulfilment and to shop. Response to the magazines' value positions will, of course, depend upon the individual – but the stereotype in the mind of adults who have not attended to the magazines carefully might well be an inaccurate one.

Teenage girls' magazines offer a very particular kind of reading experience, but it is textually quite rich, potentially educative and, given the large number of readers, clearly fulfilling. Obviously, there are limitations to what is being demanded of the reader. The reader is, for example, no longer given the chance to read the more sustained prose fiction which used to be a major feature of children's magazines. However, it would be inaccurate to assume that periodical reading makes no worthwhile contribution to young people's reading development, and, given the increasing popularity of magazine reading in the 10 to 14 age group, it seems to us important to acknowledge the reading that is taking place, and to build upon it.

References

Barker, M. (1989) *Comics: Ideology, Power and the Critics*, Manchester: Manchester University Press

Barthes, R. (1977) *Image, Music, Text*, New York: Hill & Wang

Just 17, (April 1995), a UK monthly periodical published by EMAP Elan, London

McRobbie, A. (1997) 'Pecs and penises: the meaning of girlie culture' *Soundings*, issue 5, spring 1997

McRobbie, A. (1988) *Feminism and Youth Culture*, London: Macmillan

McRobbie, A. and Nava, M. (1984) *Gender and Generation*, London: Macmillan

Radway, J. (1987) *Reading the Romance: Women, Patriarchy and Popular Literature*, London: Verso

Walkerdine, V. (1987) 'No Laughing Matter: girls' comics and the preparation for adult sexuality' in Broughton, J. M. (ed.) *Theories of Psychological Development*, New York: Plenum

Winship, J. (1987) *Inside Women's Magazines*, London: Pandora

Chapter 4

Boys' and girls' reading

In this chapter, we discuss the differences between girls' and boys' reading choices and habits. We discuss favourite genres, including preferences for fiction and non-fiction, and attitudes to reading generally. We conclude with a report of interview data in which children reflect on the influence of gender on their own and their contemporaries' reading. The Endpiece to the chapter is a short discussion of gender and reading development in school.

Boys' and girls' reading habits

Girls tend to read more than boys. When asked whether they had read a book in the four weeks prior to the survey, 74.5 per cent of boys and 84.1 per cent of girls responded positively. This is not a new phenomenon. The figures reported in Table 1.2 (Chapter 1) show the consistency of trends between the 1971 Whitehead survey and the 1994 *Children's Reading Choices* survey: both indicate that girls read more than boys at each age, and that children read fewer books as they grow older. Indeed, surveys conducted in 1940, by Jenkinson, and 1955, by Himmelweit, indicated the same pattern. Himmelweit summed up her findings on this matter thus: 'Girls read more than boys, younger children read more than adolescents (their books may be shorter), and those of high intelligence more than the less intelligent' (p. 323) Girls re-read more than boys do and are more likely than boys to leave a book unfinished (Tables 4.1 and 4.2).

There are significant differences in the types of books chosen by boys and girls (Tables 4.3 and 4.4). As a proportion of their total reading diet, girls read comparatively more adventure, horror/ghost, animal- and school-related stories and slightly more poetry. The differences are even more significant in relation to books about relationships and romance. The most marked difference between girls' and boys' choices relates to this last category. A greater percentage of boys' reading is science fiction and fantasy, sports-related books and war and spy stories. More boys read comic and joke books, annuals and humorous fiction. Interestingly, crime

Table 4.1 Re-reading by sex

Number of books re-read	Boys as % of category	Girls as % of category
0	54.2	45.8
1	46.4	53.6
2	47.0	53.0
3	41.4	58.6

Table 4.2 Unfinished books by sex

Number of unfinished books	Boys as % of category	Girls as % of category
0	52.8	47.2
1	46.4	53.6
2	37.6	62.4
3	53.7	46.3

Table 4.3 Reading of book types within each sex

Book type	% boys having read a book in this category in the last four weeks	% girls having read a book in this category in the last four weeks
Adventure	39.5	45.7
Horror/ghost	16.3	25.9
Romance/relationships	7.7	31.9
Animal related	14.5	21.0
Science fiction/fantasy	16.7	8.0
Comedy	9.7	5.9
Crime/detective	5.7	5.6
Sports related	7.7	1.8
School	3.4	6.1
War/spy related	4.6	1.7
Poetry	2.1	3.4

Table 4.4 Reading of each book type across sexes

Book type	Boys as % of readers	Girls as % of readers
Adventure	47.8	52.2
Horror/ghost	40.0	60.0
Romance/relationships	20.3	79.7
Animal related	42.2	57.8
Science fiction/fantasy	68.9	31.1
Comedy	63.4	36.6
Crime/detective	51.4	48.6
Sports related	82.1	17.9
School related	36.8	63.2
War/spy related	74.1	25.9
Poetry	39.5	60.5

and detective works are relatively evenly balanced in their popularity as a proportion of the reading diet of both sexes. This stands out as the only such book type in the *Children's Reading Choices* survey.

We have reported earlier (Chapter 1, Table 1.5) the finding that most 10- to 14-year-olds had been reading children's and teenage fiction in the month prior to the survey, and that only a small percentage of the sample had been concentrating exclusively on non-fiction texts. These 'reader type' figures show up interesting differences between boys and girls. Although only 2.8 per cent of the total sample read exclusively non-fiction, 78 per cent of those who do are boys. Boys are more likely to be in the 'hybrid' category (i.e. reading books from more than one category), probably because of a greater taste for some non-fiction in their reading diet. They are also more likely to be readers of exclusively 'adult' fiction; girls are more likely to be readers of children's and teenage fiction. As reported earlier (in Chapter 2), girls are more voracious readers of series books than boys are; girls are also very likely to be reading the same periodicals (see Chapter 3). Whilst the general trend, therefore, is towards greater diversification in reading as children grow older, it is also the case that more girls than boys share a canon of popular books and magazines. The social and cultural implications of this include the obvious, and, it seems to us, significant one: that girls share more reference points than boys do for group discussion and conversation about stories and issues raised in the course of their reading, and that this fact influences group behaviours related to literacy.

Table 4.5 Reader types by sex

Reader type	% within that type: boys	% within that type: girls
Children's fiction	43.1	56.9
Adult fiction	57.0	43.0
Non-fiction	77.9	22.1
Hybrid	54.6	45.4

Attitudes to reading

Significantly more girls than boys (73.5 per cent compared to 57.5 per cent) expressed positive attitudes to reading when asked to complete the sentence 'I think that reading is . . .'. Girls are more likely to see the educational benefits of reading than boys and are more likely to think of reading as a leisure pursuit.

There is also a marked difference between the amounts of reading girls and boys engage in, by their own assessment. Only 29.6 per cent of boys, compared to 47.5 per cent of girls, judged that they read 'quite a lot' or 'a large amount'.

Table 4.6 Children's view of reading by sex

	Positive (%)	Neutral (%)	Negative (%)	Educational (%)	Good pastime (%)	Other (%)
Boys	47.1	27.7	13.9	7.5	2.9	0.9
Girls	59.2	20.7	5.2	8.9	5.4	0.7

Both girls and boys are positive about their abilities as readers, but girls are more positive than boys: 62.7 per cent of girls and 55.8 per cent of boys consider themselves good or very good readers. These attitudes to reading were borne out in the interview phase of the *Children's Reading Choices* project. Some children, usually the older ones, adopted a fairly utilitarian view of the personal benefits of reading:

It helps my English and vocab. (Girl, 14)

Others, mainly girls, articulated their sense of escape through literature:

You can have your own imagination with books and you can picture it in your own way. (Girl, 10)

I like to go off into my own world. (Girl, 14)

I like to visualise for myself the characters in the books. (Girl, 14)

Table 4.7 Children's perceptions of the amount they read by sex

Amount of reading	% boys	% girls
A large amount	10.0	18.0
Quite a lot	19.6	29.5
About average	36.4	32.9
Not very much	23.0	14.5
Only a little	11.1	5.0

Table 4.8 Children's perceptions of their own reading ability by sex

View of reading ability	% boys	% girls
Very good	20.2	22.2
Good	35.6	40.5
Average	33.1	29.4
Not very good	9.0	6.4
Poor	2.0	1.5

Many of the girls talked about their identification with a family or community in the books they read. This theme was much less notable in the boys' comments.

[On Gerald Durrell]: Oh, it's wonderful, the Corfu ones especially, I like the family, he really describes them so funnily because they're a very eccentric family. Oh, at the beginning, it's just so wonderful, it's Corfu before the war, he describes it so well, it's really poetic, the first bits of the chapters. It makes you want to fly there. I liked the *Secret Seven* books, some Dick King-Smith and oh yeah, the *William* books, I still read those, they're brilliant. I changed to Gerald Durrell because I loved him. I also read other books, like the Willard Price books. (Girl, 10)

I've got loads of favourites but the *Babysitter* books and books by Enid Blyton, Anne Fine and Roald Dahl are good. The *Babysitters Club* tells you all about people babysitting for other children and they get money and put it to good use and they have sleep overs and parties and playschools. I still enjoy reading the other books. (Girl, 10)

It would have to be Judy Blume again, *Are You There God? It's Me Margaret*. It's definitely my favourite. It's really realistic about how girls grow up and friendships and moving into a new town. And the way she relates to her parents and her new friends. It's just the way she does it . . . Margaret . . . and she speaks to God every night about what happened in the day. When she's angry with her parents and shouts at them, she speaks to God . . . but she doesn't actually believe in God and she doesn't know which religion she believes in and she can't decide. Her parents don't believe in any religion because they just want to be normal, they don't really want any religion. She talks to God but she doesn't actually believe in any religion which I think is really good. (Girl, 10)

Dawn's Big Date by Babysitters. I liked the character of Dawn and the story. I understood the way she felt sometimes. (Girl, 10)

The book that I really really like is the one I'm reading now, it's *The Diary of Anne Frank*. It's just so moving and I saw the video of her last week and it just made me cry, just like the book. (Girl, 10)

I used to like Judy Blume because she wrote things about my age group and how I feel . . . like true stories . . . like real life stories. (Girl, 12)

Interview with the Vampire is really good and you really feel for him. (Girl, 14)

> In *The Secret Diary of Adrian Mole* you can relate to the storyline.
> (Girl, 14)

> *Teacher's Pet* is a great book, the main character is like me, I felt for her.
> (Girl, 14)

> You can relate to the love story in *Forever Young*, the relationship
> between the characters and their feelings. (Girl, 14)

Boys often emphasised independence and autonomy, giving a sense of
a somewhat detached but interested relationship to the subject matter and
style of the book.

> I like Ian Livingstone, *Fighting Fantasy*, because you choose what you
> do, sort of like if you want to fight a monster or something, it's like
> life. When the monster hits you, you sort of deduct stamina or skill.
> (Boy, 10)

> I'm reading *Iron Man* at the moment and I really like that, it's by Ted
> Hughes I think. It's sort of like fantasy, I like made up stuff. The
> storyline is good. (Boy, 10)

> *Homing Pigeon.* It's got some pictures of some good birds and some
> people have had their huts burnt down because they've won so many
> races. (Boy, 10)

> I like Jeffrey Archer because he writes good, enjoyable books with
> brilliant storylines. I used to like Stephen King because I liked horror
> but I started to enjoy more realistic and true to life stories. (Boy, 12)

> *The Hobbit* has an excellent storyline, it's weird and makes you think
> what you would do. (Boy, 12)

> I only like true life books, I go to my aunt's house, she has a whole
> load of fictional books where the main points in the book are actually
> taken from real life. Where she lives, there's been a book written
> about gangsters, warfare around that bit and it's been put into a story.
> (Boy, 14)

> I like *Star Trek* and any science fiction to do with space. I'm very
> interested in space travel and time travel and things like that. I used to
> like some of the magician type stories, when I was younger. I used
> to like Hans Christian Andersen, I liked some of the stuff he did. I'm
> usually a mixed person, I don't usually stick with one author, I
> usually mix around. *Star Trek* was the one that attracted me, I could
> eat, live, breathe *Star Trek*. (Boy, 14)

Many interviewees, especially girls, had a sense of the desirability of
reading at their own level:

I don't mind the Babysitter books, I like Betsy Byars, she's good, I don't know why but she caters for young, middle aged and quite older kids. I think she's not serious, she has some serious books and there are funny bits. I like the way she's made these characters, they're not like real people, human beings, because they do all these weird things. I used to like Anne Fine, I gone off her because I read *Bill's New Frock* and *The Flour Babies*, I found them quite boring, they didn't have much liveliness in them, they were a bit slow I thought. I liked them first of all because they were easy to read but now they're too easy and boring. (Girl, 10)

I think Judy Blume, I've only read one of her books but I really like the way she explains it. And our teacher read some of her books to us. She's really good at expressing what they're feeling. When I was younger, I used to like Roald Dahl. I used to read all his books. I've got *Fantastic Mr Fox* and *Charlie and the Chocolate Factory*. I used to read Enid Blyton, both Enid Blyton and Roald Dahl. I used to like the fairy tales. I changed because I found them a bit babyish after a while and I wanted to read bigger books and more up to date books. I just found them a bit unrealistic. When you're younger you like that kind of stuff. (Girl, 10)

Others, often boys, were less confident about their abilities to sustain pace and concentration:

I think they're too long really. You get a book and it takes you days and days to read it, you get bored after a while. (Boy, 10)

Books are too long. (Boy, 14)

I've got too much coursework. (Boy, 14)

For both boys and girls, friends and media tie-ins are important motivational factors for beginning a book:

Say one of my friends read it and they said it was really good then I'd maybe read it. (Girl, 10)

If it was exciting or something or if lots of people talked about it and spread rumours and things like that. (Girl, 12)

Roald Dahl, that's my favourite one, probably because all the books I really like are Roald Dahl – *Charlie and the Chocolate Factory* – because they're . . . yes, they're exciting. I used to like Dick King-Smith. I changed because when I knew other friends were reading them and reading in the classroom. They were like more exciting and I tried to get all the books that they'd been reading and like saying, 'Can I borrow them?' and because they'd said they were good. And I like them. (Boy, 10)

Well, what it's about, say it was about Mrs Doubtfire, I've seen the film so I'd probably get the book. Just if I've heard something about it or at school or I've seen it on TV. (Boy, 10)

Reading non-fiction

The interview data indicate that there are gender-specific patterns in attitudes towards reading non-fiction. For example, all of the 12-year-old boys interviewed maintained that they enjoyed reading non-fiction, whereas most of the 14-year-old girls said that they found it boring and difficult to read. The boys tended to equate non-fiction with an excitement about finding out about 'the real world'. On the other hand, several girls expressed the view that non-fiction 'doesn't require any imagination' and they would prefer to use TV documentaries or CD ROMs as sources of information. This topic is discussed in more detail in the Endpiece to the current chapter.

> I don't like them as much as I like fiction books. I don't find them interesting but I don't mind some of them, it's just that I can't get into them. I try reading them but I couldn't read a whole book. I can only read like what I'm looking for to find a fact or something but I don't really like them very much because they're not exciting, they're just facts facts facts and stuff like that. I need something exciting in my books so that I can get into them. (Girl, 10)

> About animals they're good, about their habitat and all that and what they do out hunting and playing and eating and all. (Boy, 10)

> Yes, I like them because they're like true and sometimes for information. (Boy, 10)

> I like my fishing book best of all because it is so useful. (Boy, 12)

> I won't read them often. They're interesting if I'm doing a project but they get a bit boring . . . just reading facts. Information books with pictures like those Dorling Kindersley ones, they're really nice to look at. If I see something that grabs my attention, then I'll really look at it but I won't think oh I'll read this book. (Girl, 12)

> I am interested in horses and you have to know the practical details. (Girl, 14)

> I do like atlases. It has useful information on the different cultures.

What I think it basically is, is that you end up learning something at the end and it's fun at the same time. (Boy, 14)

Children's views on gender influences on reading

We were keen to use the interview phase of the project to engage the children in thinking about some of the key issues that were emerging in the research. The interviewer therefore explained to interviewees that the questionnaires showed that girls read more than boys, and she asked them to try to account for this finding.

The young people's answers reveal a very high degree of agreement about the reasons why boys show less interest in reading: football specifically (and sport generally), the influence of image and peer culture, and differences in boys' and girls' inclination towards physical activity. In addition to these reasons, many girls thought that they were more mature than their male counterparts, and that this made them more inclined to read; other, older girls expressed the view that girls are emotionally better suited to reading.

Both boys and girls at 10+ think that the main reason that boys do not read as much as girls is that they are too busy playing football.

Boys like football! I don't know really because we have a quiet reading session and I think girls are reading and the boys can't be bothered and they're talking. I don't know why boys don't read, I think it's just that they prefer to do other things than just to sit and be quiet and read. (Girl, 10)

Most boys just like playing out and playing football and that. (Girl, 10)

Some boys probably think that reading is boring, they usually do. They think about football, yes, usually football. They don't really have to but girls probably just like reading books and boys probably think, oh! girls are reading, it's probably girlie. (Girl, 10)

Girls see themselves as being more mature and able to apply themselves to reading. At 12+, both girls and boys introduced the concept of image, some children stating that boys regard reading as being 'sissy'. At 14+ both girls and boys recognised that girls read more than boys, and each group attributed this mainly to the boys' interest in sport and a preference to do other things. Almost half of the girls felt that they were naturally more inclined to read because they were well suited to reading emotionally. This view was supported by one boy. Generally, however, the consensus amongst interviewees was remarkable; we therefore end this part of the chapter with a selection of the children's views.

Boys can't sit still, they fidget and they're always running about doing some kind of sport. (Girl, 10)

Girls are more mature and they find more time to read. (Girl, 10)

Girls are not as active as boys. They stay in to read and to talk to their friends. (Boy, 10)

Boys are too busy going out and playing football. We're too busy mucking about. (Boy, 10)

They don't have much to do, they don't like much, they just like going out, like doing skipping and that, they don't have much to do. Some girls play football, but the lasses don't have much to do really. The boys, we play football, go on bike rides, climb trees, climb walls and get into trouble, hop fences and all that. (Boy, 10)

Well . . . boys often, they go out more don't they? They play football and that and they don't have as much time. It might not be considered to be cool to read. Well there are more books for girls than boys I think . . . Although you go out with your friends, it's not as much as boys. You don't kick a ball around or anything, it's not arranged. A lot of teenage books . . . people just enjoy really. (Girl, 12)

Boys prefer football and being out and about . . . or playing computer games or dossing about with their friends (like my brother). Most girls would prefer to read when there's nothing to do. Quiet girls may help their parents in the house. (Girl, 12)

I don't know really, maybe because boys prefer sport. They probably think it's a bit sissy to read. (Girl, 12)

Boys are more active and more sporty, more adventurous. They like to be outdoors doing a lot more. Girls don't have as much to do, they just like to go to their friends to read and chat. (Boy, 12)

Boys who read are called squares and are goody-goodies. (Boy, 12)

Boys can't be bothered to read, they've got no patience. (Girl, 14)

It's obvious, boys have football. They think reading is wet. Boys have to act cool and they're sexist and think reading is puffy. (Girl, 14)

Girls are more sensitive and more romantic. More soppy. (Girl, 14)

Boys have got this tough image of trying to act cool in front of their friends and going out late and staying up and never doing any homework or class work. I think it's just an ego thing really. I think that boys do read when they're on their own but when their friends are there they deny it actually, because I think everybody needs to read. Because I think girls, I think they mature a lot quicker than boys. I think girls have a lot more of an open nature to reading and education than boys do because boys have got this bad boy image. (Girl, 14)

Boys are more sociable than girls. They just stay in. (Boy,14)

Girls seem to be better, girls seem to enjoy reading more, I don't really know why. They like bigger books about love and that kind of thing. (Boy, 14)

I'm not always with my mates, I don't read all of the time like, but sometimes when I come in, it's like huh! reading again like and they start mucking around. It's difficult to explain really, they think it's puffy or too girlie and some people like get the mick taken out of them. Boys are meant to be strong and muck around. Well, girls tend to be more emotional than boys, they usually read and they're more interested in other things. (Boy, 14)

Summary

- Girls read and re-read more than boys do.
- The different sexes tend to favour different genres of books; only crime and detective works are fairly evenly balanced in their readership across the sexes.
- Few children read non-fiction exclusively, but those that do tend to be boys.
- Many girls share a canon of series books and periodicals as they grow older, and therefore, in comparison with boys, have more texts in common to discuss.
- Girls have more positive attitudes to reading than boys do.
- Many girls and boys can articulate clearly the influence of gender on reading. They emphasise particularly the increasing importance of peer group activities and expectations in determining girls' and boys' reading habits.

Endpiece: gender, reading development and school

The *Children's Reading Choices* research findings confirm that reading patterns and practices are highly gendered, and that they become increasingly gender specific as children move into adolescence. Teachers and parents observe this on a routine basis. The difficulties for adults concerned with children's reading development stem not so much from observing the trends, as from knowing what to do about them: deciding when, how or if to intervene in the interests of broadening the range or increasing the complexity of texts. In the brief discussion which follows, we consider teachers' responsibilities for reading development, arguing that teachers need to understand boys' and girls' reading choices in order to build upon them and help both sexes develop as critical readers.

A joint publication from the Equal Opportunities Commission and OFSTED, *The Gender Divide*, reports that in England girls are more successful than boys at every level in examinations at 16. In the three core subjects of English, mathematics and science, English is notable in that girls out-perform boys at each of the assessment stages (7, 11, 14 and 16). A report from Her Majesty's Inspectorate entitled *Boys and English* published in 1993 pointed out that boys' attitudes towards reading and writing tend to be more negative than girls': 'They often have narrower experiences of fiction, write more predictably, and have difficulty with the affective aspects of English' (OFSTED, 1993). Boys' standards of achievement are often linked in the popular press to a supposed fall in reading standards, and boys' reading particularly has been a recent focus for concern.

The book choices of boys surveyed in the *Children's Reading Choices* project suggest that many boys are making an early entry into a stereotypical male world of technical invention, action, machinery and hard objects. The survey also shows that boys' *book* reading is primarily narrative. This is counter to the prevalent conception in England that boys are interested primarily in non-fiction books. In the 1970s boys increasingly read non-fiction books as they got older. Now when non-fiction is read the readers are mainly boys, but overwhelmingly both boys' and girls' book reading at all ages is narrative fiction. It seems that boys' appetite for non-fiction is being fed by periodicals.

The category 'non-fiction' is problematic however. There is, in the most popular periodicals, factual information, for example about real aspects of sports culture, but there is also a fictionalised element constituted by the particular placement of the reader in relation to sports heroes and pop stars, who are often portrayed in a way which feeds the imagination and fantasies of young readers. Invented stories from 'facts' are an increasing element in our culture, evidenced for instance by popular television programmes which use police film footage from surveillance cameras to create stories, and 'faction' or 'fictionographies'. Many boys' enjoyment of narrative is perhaps via this genre of invented stories from facts, particularly in magazines. Where boys are choosing this kind of material, which offers them one way into narrative, it is surely important to build upon it: to use 'faction' within the school reading curriculum to encourage and sustain reading development. In our view any reading programme should include within it the intention to help pupils become critical in their non-fiction reading, to understand that information in books and magazines is never value neutral, and to recognise the particular agendas of the authors and publishers of non-fiction. Boys' reading of football and computer magazines, with their dense information-packed formats, offers a starting point for this work, but one which is not always clearly recognised in classrooms. By taking insufficient account of this voluntary reading, school reading programmes miss opportunities to help boys develop their reading of the sorts of challenging factual texts they often prefer, and have developed some facility in reading.

It is now commonplace to point to the predominantly 'female' culture of primary classrooms. Certainly in the primary school high-status literacy activities are most often carried out by women, there is a shortage of male role models, and the classroom often resembles a domestic environment. The encouraging findings from the *Children's Reading Choices* project with regard to younger children's interest in reading suggest that this is a successful context for early reading development. In the secondary school if boys are particularly anxious to discover and define themselves in ways which are different to girls, one way to do this is to resist or oppose the prevailing culture. If girls seem to demonstrate being comfortable and in tune with school expectations, one of which will be a strong interest in literacy activities, then older boys may in part be reacting against the contexts for reading. There are practical ways of altering these contexts: many teachers could take children's voluntary reading choices more seriously, they could broaden definitions of what counts as being 'a good reader' by careful analysis of what readers can, rather than what they cannot do, and they could work with pupils to help them see the kind of reader they are and to make choices about the kind of reader they would like to become.

To say this is not to say that teachers ought to, for example, construct their teaching in a way which simplistically 'panders' to boys' interests. It is to suggest that all pupils can be taken forward in their reading habits and understanding if they are encouraged to take a critical perspective on their own reading diet, and if they are helped to see how as readers they are constructed by the culture. This might happen, for instance, if pupils were asked to reflect on their own reading histories and how they had come to have the tastes they have, or if there was more discussion in classrooms about how children might negotiate their own paths through the consumerism or the moral and ethical issues which are raised in and by their magazines. It might happen if there was more recognition within the reading curriculum that reading magazines might not be a light and trivial pursuit, but might assist a reader in becoming more skilled or discerning.

These arguments apply equally to girls' reading, which, by contrast with boys' reading, has in recent times been seen as relatively unprob-lematic. The *Children's Reading Choices* project shows clearly that girls' book reading choices are overwhelmingly dominated by narrative fiction, both in their individual and shared reading. The trend towards shared reading of series titles amongst girls brings with it many positive features: not least, discussion of the characters and textual features, consideration of moral and ethical issues, and, obviously, enjoyment. The primary focus in this reading is likely to be an inward looking one: using literacy to cement values, create group cultures, and function as an aspect of social discourse – all of which are highly valuable.

Girls' magazines, like their counterparts for boys, contain significant amounts of non-fiction in the form of information, advice and bio-graphical detail. This non-fiction is presented in a similar manner in both boys' and girls' magazines, in that it is mediated by a clear narrative frame. Information and advice are passed on through story, and character details and preferences support the bias towards narrative which is so evident in the girls' choice of books. But in the boys' magazines there is also an assumption that the reader will be interested in statistical and technological information; there is no corresponding assumption about the female readers. The range of reading demands is in some ways broader than in the girls' magazines. The consequence of this is that boys are practising reading technological information, numbers, instructions and factual reports far more routinely than girls are.

Several implications arise from this. First, there is the matter of ensuring that girls are given a proper breadth in the range of reading required of them in school: if they are not choosing to encounter this type of reading in their leisure time, then it is important that schools see their role in terms of equipping girls with the necessary confidence and competence to approach technological and factual reading positively. In the current climate of particular concern about boys' reading this aspect of girls' reading development is easily overlooked.

The second major point is about the conceptualisation of what it is to be literate and 'a good reader' within the school curriculum. Too close an association between literacy and the subject English has resulted in reading becoming overly associated with personal response, empathetic and autobiographical work and, overwhelmingly, with narrative prose fiction. We are not in any sense arguing against the value of this work but want to point up some of the consequences of adopting too narrow a notion of literacy within the English secondary school system. One consequence is that, since teenage boys' culture in England tends to take as one of its central predicates the notion that speaking publicly about your emotions is the very antithesis of being stylish, there is often some discomfort for boys around the dominant modes of working being employed. This may well be a generally productive discomfort. Where it is less productive, we are arguing, is where it results in boys feeling that their preferred modes of reading are not valued in school and indeed that their own reading is discounted in some way. It was not at all uncommon in the interview phase of the *Children's Reading Choices* project to come across boys who had created for themselves reference libraries of, for example, football programmes which they regularly referred to, read and re-read. These boys often viewed themselves as non-readers. Whilst we are not proposing that the reading of football programmes should be regarded as a literacy standard to aspire to, it is nonetheless a start, and a positive one in comparison with seeing yourself as someone who does not read at all. Just over one-third (34 per cent) of boys in the *Children's Reading Choices* survey considered that they 'didn't do much reading'. The first, essential, conceptual move for these boys is to help them see themselves as readers: to build a view of the kind of reader they might become, and therefore, crucially, of the range of choices they have and the possibilities for self-directed development and diversification.

The corollary of this, of course, is that girls report spending more time reading than boys do, and their attitudes to reading are more positive than boys' – 73.5 per cent of girls responded positively about their attitudes towards reading in comparison with 57.5 per cent of boys. Whilst acknowledging the success of teachers in promoting and sustaining reading habits amongst girls, it seems important to recognise the virtuous circle which is dominating patterns here. Cultural influences on girls are encouraging them to read and value narrative; school definitions of English and reading reinforce those patterns; girls feel positive and successful in these terms and tend to have relatively high self-esteem about their reading and to do relatively well in English examinations. But is this enough? We are arguing that it is not; that school definitions of literacy are slow to change, and that the literacies of subjects other than English are paid insufficient attention in the school curriculum. They are correspondingly insufficiently assessed and rewarded at examination level.

For both girls and boys, we need to pay closer attention to the range of literacy skills they are developing out of school to ensure that school is used to supplement and extend skills and help individual readers develop greater range. We cannot afford to be complacent about girls' reading or to adopt simplistic approaches towards attempting to meet the needs of one sex (at the moment boys) in isolation from the habits and experiences of the other sex. The issues for both are closely entwined, and they need to be considered in terms of the broader cultural influences on young people's leisure-time reading, and the real working definitions of literacy and reading that we are employing within the education system at this time of immense change in the technologies of literacy.

Clearly, reading teaching must challenge pupils of both sexes. All good teaching must assist children's performances, must help them move from where they are now, via tasks which can only be tackled with the help of an adult or more capable peer, to the next step in their development. Simply providing texts which match pupils' current interests will not move them forward in those interests. It is important to acknowledge a child's interests and abilities and gender, but it is important also to exercise professional responsibility to support the child's development.

The HMI report *Boys and English* notes that: 'When reading was taught well and pupils' private reading successfully encouraged, the distinctions between girls' and boys' reading interests were less sharp than usual' (OFSTED, 1993). We wish to argue that well-taught reading involves acknowledging and focusing on difference: gender difference, change over time and difference in literacy forms and practices. There is a need for positive teaching of individual reading based not just on differences in ability but on recognition of other differences between pupils as well, a most significant one being gender differences. Such teaching has to be based on actual enquiry into the differences between boys' and girls' reading habits rather than on stereotypical received views. It has to be based on a careful analysis of needs and interests, and a monitoring of differences in attitudes and experiences. Pupils need to be involved in discussing these differences with their teachers so that they can develop their sense of how they have been constructed as individual readers, of how some forms of reading carry greater cultural and social capital, of the levels of skill and concentration needed to engage in different types of reading, of the purposes and implied audiences for different texts. It is only by opening up the discussion to include children and by taking their tastes more seriously that we can help to create critical and discerning readers. And critical and discerning readers are the ones who will be instrumental in deconstructing current highly gendered reading profiles.

References

Equal Opportunities Commission and OFSTED (1996) *The Gender Divide: Performance Differences between Boys and Girls at School* London: HMSO

Jenkinson, A. J. (1940) *What Do Boys and Girls Read?* London: Methuen

OFSTED (1993) *Boys and English: a Report from the Office of Her Majesty's Chief Inspector of Schools*, London: DFEE (ref 2/93/NS)

Whitehead, F. *et al.* (1977) *Children and Their Books: the Final Report of the Schools Council Research Project on Children's Reading Habits*, 10–15, London: Macmillan

Chapter 5

The influence of family background

In this chapter we set out the *Children's Reading Choices* project findings related to socio-economic background, ethnicity and reading. We consider these factors with reference to amounts of reading and reading preferences. Later in the chapter we consider the importance to children's reading of living with adults who are perceived as keen readers, and the importance of living with siblings who read. The chapter concludes with a consideration of the survey findings related to children who speak languages additional to English.

The *Children's Reading Choices* survey findings are analysed in terms of sex, age, socio-economic group and ethnicity. As one would expect, these last two categories are problematic in terms of reliability, particularly as we depended upon self-report from the children. Socio-economic groupings were labelled A, B, C_1, C_2, D/E categorised in accordance with the Registrar General's classification (see Appendix 2), which is based on the occupation of head of household. Children themselves designated the occupation of the adults they live with and clearly those designations are open to interpretation in terms of the classification. The accuracy of some children's knowledge about their parents' occupations was also somewhat suspect; a significant number of children, for example, recorded simply that their parent 'worked in an office'. The normal caveats which would apply to any categorisation of people into socio-economic groups therefore need to be applied even more carefully in relation to this part of the survey findings.

It is also difficult to arrive at clear information and definitions regarding children's ethnicity. Children's self-report on this necessarily openly phrased question means that the data may be compromised, in an area of investigation which is anyway open to debate and discussion. In fact 4.5 per cent of the sample did not provide information on ethnicity. The categories we worked with (see Appendix 2) were those used at the time by the Council for Racial Equality. The range of minority groups we ended up with was so large, and the numbers within each group were so small, that for the purposes of the analysis we identified two broad categories: those who identified themselves as 'white', and those who identified themselves as members of other groups. The importance of considering ethnicity in relation to children's book choices has led us to maintain this less than satisfactory categorisation in order to see if any interesting findings emerged which could then be tracked back to the different ethnic groupings.

Amount of reading

The *Children's Reading Choices* findings indicate, as might be expected, that socio-economic circumstances and family background are highly significant factors in children's reading choices and habits. This is most starkly illustrated by the findings related to the amount that different children read. It is important to note, however, that these differences relate to socio-economic grouping, and not to ethnicity. There is no significant difference between the amounts of reading that children of different ethnic groupings are engaged in. However, there is a clear pattern of decline in the amount of book reading from more to less advantaged socio-economic groups; children from more advantaged socio-economic groups are more likely than those from less advantaged groups to have read a book in the previous month, as can be seen from Table 5.1.

The average number of books read in the month prior to the survey by children in each socio-economic group is shown in Table 5.2. Since the numbers of books which children say they own declines steadily from social group A to social group D/E, and since analysis of periodical purchase suggests a pattern of buying limited only by purchasing power (see Chapter 6 for a report on both of these aspects), it is likely that the findings are explained as much by economic as by cultural factors. These findings about amounts of reading and social class might be considered alongside studies such as the NFER's *Reading in Recession* (1992), which concluded that there had been a small but significant drop in the reading performance of pupils in the decade prior to its publication, but that lower

Table 5.1 Reading of any book in the previous month by socio-economic group

Social group	% 'Yes' responses
Group A	87.6
Group B	84 3
Group C$_1$	78.2
Group C$_2$	77.0
Group D/E	75.9

standards were not general. Thirty-seven per cent of the schools in the NFER sample had raised their scores. All of these were schools in shire counties, rural areas or in middle-class suburbs of larger conurbations; the link between social class, poverty and reading performance is notable in this research. More recent analysis of the attainment of literacy by two cohorts of people born in 1958 and 1970 (Robinson, 1997) emphasises the dominant impact of economic disadvantage. The evidence from these longitudinal studies is that such factors as class size, teaching methods, the use of streaming and setting in schools and even pre-school education, fade into insignificance compared with the detrimental effects of poverty. We therefore point out what should perhaps be obvious: that in drawing conclusions from reports such as the *Children's Reading Choices* project we must look at the circumstances of economic need and social disadvantage in which too many children live.

Table 5.2 Average number of books read in the month prior to the survey by socio-economic group

A	B	C_1	C_2	D/E
2.92	2.84	2.49	2.46	2.40

Reading preferences

The list of favourite authors can be considered in relation to the socio-economic grouping of the readers, though clearly the figures are more reliable for the more widely read authors. Roald Dahl, for example, is most popular amongst socio-economic group C_2, followed by D/E and C_1. group. Enid Blyton's popularity increases as one moves down the social scale. Point Horror is named by far more girls than boys as a favourite and by a higher percentage of social group A than any other. Judy Blume is more likely to be named as a favourite in social group A, although generally her appeal seems to be consistent across socio-economic groups. Stephen King becomes more popular with older children and a higher percentage of boys than girls across all social groups. Francine Pascal's following is largest in group C1, amongst girls at 12+ particularly. Terry Pratchett is most popular amongst boys of 12 and 14+, with a higher percentage of readership in social groups B and A. Dick King-Smith is named fairly evenly by both sexes as their favourite author, with higher percentages from the youngest of our age groups and in socio-economic group A. The *Babysitters Club* and *Fighting Fantasy* series are highly gender related, to girls and boys respectively, but across all social groups. Both of these series are most popular amongst 12+ year olds.

The statistics relating socio-economic group and favourite authors are not generally notable at the lower end of the 'top 30' list, but certain points seem worthy of comment. Sue Townsend, J. R. R. Tolkien, Robin Jarvis and Douglas Adams have a higher percentage of mentions in groups A and B. Christopher Pike has the highest percentage in group D/E, as does Charles Dickens, who is not named as favourite amongst the A group. The numbers of mentions are, however, small when this part of the list is divided into socio-economic groups.

Table 5.3 sets out the findings on book types as they pertain to broad socio-economic groupings. In socio-economic group A, therefore, adventure and horror stories are fairly evenly balanced in the children's reading diet as a whole. This is not the case amongst the other social groups. As one moves down the social scale, the balance between the amount of adventure being read and the amount of horror is increasingly tipped in favour of the former. Children in social group D/E have a fairly evenly balanced amount of romance, animal-related and science fiction books amongst their choices. In groups A, B and C_1 there is a more marked preference for stories of romance and relationships.

Table 5.3 Reading of each book type within socio-economic groups

Book type	% readers within group A	% readers within group B	% readers within group C_1	% readers within group C_2	% readers within group D/E
Adventure	36.4	40.7	38.9	45.6	48.9
Horror	31.3	26.0	22.7	19.8	18.3
Romance	22.4	25.9	21.4	17.8	13.9
Animal	12.5	16.8	18.1	18.7	15.1
Sci-fi	14.7	16.5	12.5	9.9	12.6
Comedy	8.0	7.3	7.3	7.4	8.2
Crime	9.9	9.1	5.1	3.4	4.1
Sports	5.4	3.9	4.6	5.9	7.3
School	3.5	4.8	5.1	4.4	5.0
War	4.2	4.9	2.7	3.1	2.2
Poetry	1.9	2.5	2.0	3.9	3.8
Other non-fiction	8.0	6.2	6.4	6.6	8.5
Other fiction	1.9	2.1	2.8	4.3	3.2
Unclassifiable	1.0	2.5	2.8	3.4	3.5

It is interesting to note where the variation across socio-economic groups is least. It is notable, for instance, that the category 'comedy' is one that is read more or less equally within each of the social groups. For school- and animal-related books there are also no very significant differences between the reading habits of children in different groups, although both types of book are read less by children in socio-economic group A than by children in other groups.

The categories which show a very significant skew towards one or other end of the social scale are 'poetry', 'crime/detective' and 'horror/ghost' texts. Although there is not much poetry reading going on, we can see that not only is poetry reading more popular amongst younger children, but also children from lower socio-economic groups (D/E and C_2) are proportionately more likely to be reading it. However, it is worth noting that Roald Dahl's *Revolting Rhymes* was the only poetry book to come in the top one hundred favourite titles. One explanation for the appeal of poetry to younger children might relate to the fact that poems stand as discrete, short texts which can be encompassed by a younger child or weaker reader in one reading.

The reading of crime and detective books is, on the other hand, skewed towards children in the highest socio-economic groups, and declines significantly in popularity outside those groups. Since detective stories usually require a degree of fluency that involves a more than usual amount of reading between the lines, or inferential comprehension, these stories are likely to appeal to the more able readers in the survey sample.

Contrary to what many teachers might imagine, horror and ghost stories are most popular amongst children from the highest socio-economic groups declining in popularity as one moves through the social classes. Adventure books are popular throughout the socio-economic groups. Science fiction and fantasy is also most popular amongst socio-economic group B, although the spread of readers is fairly even, with a dip in social class C_2. Sports-related books are most widely read in socio-economic group D/E and thereafter in C_2 and A, and clearly therefore appeal to an interestingly diverse range of readers.

It is notable too that amongst the higher socio-economic groups the percentages of 'adult fiction' readers are larger than for other reader types (Table 5.4). The high figure for non-fiction readers in the 'D/E' group is also notable, although the numbers involved are small. The largest percentage of 'hybrid' readers, that is readers who we found to be reading a range of book types, are to be found in group B.

Table 5.4 Percentage reader type within socio-economic groups

Reader type	Children's fiction	Adult fiction	Non-fiction	Hybrid	Unclassified
Group A	52.7	20.1	2.2	12.1	12.8
Group B	46.4	15.2	2.3	19.6	16.5
Group C_1	49.1	11.7	2.2	15.6	21.4
Group C_2	52.5	6.5	3.2	15.6	22.3
Group D/E	48.6	7.3	4.1	15.8	24.3

It is possible to fill out the picture provided so far by considering the readership of some of the most popular periodicals in terms of socio-economic group (see Table 5.5). The data here suggest that boys' periodicals are more likely to be read across social groups whereas girls' magazines are read by particular social sectors. For instance, it appears that football and computer magazines and comics, which are read mainly by boys (*Match, Shoot, Manchester United, Sega Power, Dandy, Beano*) are read by roughly equal numbers in the different socio-economic groups. The girls' magazines, (*Big, Smash Hits, Mizz, More*) on the other hand, have readerships drawn from different socio-economic groups. The reading of tabloid newspapers is popular with all ages surveyed but this junior readership, like the adult counterpart, is located primarily in the lower socio-economic groups and primarily amongst males.

Table 5.5 Most popular periodicals by sex and by socio-economic group

Name	% of boys	% of girls	Readers by social group
Just 17	1.4	42.5	no sig. diff.
Big	2.1	35.0	C_1, C_2, D/E
Smash Hits	2.1	31.1	C_1, C_2, D/E
The Sun	17.7	14.2	C_1, C_2, D/E
The Beano	19.4	6.2	no sig. diff.
Match	18.1	1.5	no sig. diff.
Shoot	17.0	1.5	no sig. diff.
Shout	0.8	17.7	no sig. diff.
The Daily Mirror	9.0	7.6	C_1, C_2, D/E
Mizz	0.4	16.7	A, B
Fast Forward	1.7	14.0	C_1, C_2
News (various)	8.1	5.9	
The Dandy	10.4	2.6	no sig. diff.
Computer magazines (various)	10.8	0.4	A, B, C_1
TV Hits	0.8	10.8	C_1, C_2, D/E
The News of the World	4.3	4.2	C_2, D/E
More	0.2	7.7	A, B
Live & Kicking	0.6	6.3	C_2, D/E
The Evening Post (various)	3.6	3.2	C_1, C_2, D/E
Horse & Pony	0.2	5.9	C_1
Football (various)	4.9	0.4	C_1, C_2, D/E
Sega Power	2.6	0.1	no sig. diff.
Manchester United	2.8	1.3	no sig. diff.

Generally, none of the findings related to reading preferences had any significant relationship to children's ethnic background. The only exception was in the 'reader type' figures, which showed that there are comparatively more readers of 'adult fiction' amongst the children who designated themselves as 'white'. It is difficult to know why this might be, and the interviews offered us no clues. More significant, in our view, is the fact that, on a general level, ethnic background makes very little difference to the type of book a child chooses to read. On an individual level, of course, ethnicity like other aspects of individual identity, will be an important factor in book choice: '*Pele, His Life Story* is fascinating because it's all so true. (I'm Brazilian myself.)' (Boy, 14).

The influence of readers in the family

The two longitudinal studies mentioned previously, the 1958 National Child Development Study, and the 1970 British Cohort Survey, (Robinson, 1997) found that parental interest and involvement have a positive impact on children's developing literacy skills. This is an understanding that is at the foundation for much of the home/school liaison work which takes place in primary schools and for the various Family Literacy projects which have taken place in recent years.

Children in the *Children's Reading Choices* survey were asked to list the adults they lived with, give the sex of the person and tick a box if their perception was that the adult read a lot. Two-thirds of the sample (65.6 per cent) live with at least one adult who, in the child's view, reads a lot. More than half (56.8 per cent) of the children have a female adult, usually a mother, who reads a lot; fewer (38.2 per cent) have a male adult, usually a father, who they say reads a lot.

Our particular interest in this information relates to one aspect of the question of parental involvement in children's reading: that is, to whether those perceptions – of living with adults who are keen readers – seem to influence the children's views of themselves as readers, or tie in with any patterns of reading behaviour. We consider here the overall responses, girls' and boys' responses separately, and then relate them to the sex of the adult who seems to the child to 'read a lot'.

The association between children who live with an adult who reads a lot and children's perceptions of their own ability as readers is given in Table 5.6. These figures seem to suggest that there is very little, if any, relationship between the child's perception of his/her own reading ability and living in a home with adult readers. They suggest then, despite the consensus about the positive nature of parental involvement in children's reading on children's attitudes to reading, that an adult's interest in reading for himself or herself, and in the reading of children in the family may not coincide. Considered in relation to the sex of the child however, the findings suggest that boys who live with adults who read a lot are no more likely to regard themselves positively as readers than other boys (Table 5.7). Girls who live with adults who read a lot are slightly more likely to regard themselves in a positive light as readers (Table 5.8).

Wanting to take account of arguments about gender-related role modelling, we considered whether the sexes of the adults and children

Table 5.6 Adult family reading and children's perceptions of their own reading abilities

	Perceived as a very good reader	Perceived as a good reader	Perceived as an average reader	Perceived as not a very good reader	Perceived as a poor good reader
% living with no adults who read a lot	20.1	37.0	31.7	9.3	2.0
% living with 1+ adult who reads a lot	21.7	38.5	31.1	7.0	1.6

Table 5.7 Adult family reading and boys' perceptions of their own reading abilities

	Perceives himself as a very good reader	Perceives himself as a good reader	Perceives himself as an average reader	Perceives himself as not a very good reader	Perceives himself as a poor reader
% boys living with no adults who read a lot	19.6	36.1	32.4	10.4	1.5
% boys living with 1+ adult who reads a lot	20.6	35.4	33.5	8.2	2.3

involved might show a clearer relationship in terms of children's self-regard in relation to reading. We used the statistical information to investigate, separately, the relationship between boys who live with male and female adults who read a lot, and boys' perceptions of their own reading abilities, and the relationship between girls who live with male and female adults who read a lot, and girls' perceptions of their own reading abilities. Interestingly the sex of the adult whom the child views as a reader seems to make very little difference.

We pursued the question as to whether there is any discernible influence on children's own reading habits (as opposed to their views of themselves as readers) from the fact of living in a home with adults who

Table 5.8 Adult family reading and girls' perceptions of their own reading abilities

	Perceives herself as a very good reader	Perceives herself as a good reader	Perceives herself as an average reader	Perceives herself as not a very good reader	Perceives herself as a poor reader
% girls living with no adults who read a lot	20.9	37.8	31.1	7.7	2.5
% girls living with 1+ adult who reads a lot	22.9	41.8	28.5	5.8	1.0

Table 5.9 Association between children who live with adults who read a lot, and children's perceptions of the amount they read

	Perceived as reading a large amount	Perceived as reading quite a lot	Perceived as reading about an average amount	Perceived as reading not very much	Perceived as reading only a little
% living with no adults who read a lot	12.4	23.0	34.5	19.9	10.1
% living with 1+ adult who reads a lot	14.6	25.2	34.9	18.2	7.1

read. We therefore correlated the family information with the numbers of books the children had read in the last four weeks and the children's views of the amount they generally read (Table 5.9). We considered the information for girls and boys separately.

It appears that there is no notable difference between the amount of reading done by boys who live with adults who read a lot and boys who do not (Table 5.10). This conclusion is supported by an analysis of the relationship between the number of books listed as having been read by boys in the four weeks prior to the survey, and living with an adult who

Table 5.10 Adult family reading and boys' perceptions of the amount they read

	Perceives himself as reading a large amount	Perceives himself as reading quite a lot	Perceives himself as reading about an average amount	Perceives himself as reading not very much	Perceives himself as reading only a little
% boys living with no adults who read a lot	19.6	36.1	32.4	10.4	1.5
% boys living with 1+ adult who reads a lot	20.6	35.4	33.5	8.2	2.3

reads a lot: there is no significant relationship between the number of books read by boys, and the presence in the house of an adult who they perceive reads a lot. This holds true in the case of boys living with either male or female adults who read a lot.

The findings relating to girls are slightly different (see Table 5.11). The figures suggest that girls who live with an adult who reads a lot have a more positive view than other girls of the amount of reading that they do. However this perception is not supported by the information on actual numbers of books read in the four weeks prior to the survey. When we considered the relationship between the number of books listed as having been read by girls in the four weeks prior to the survey, and living with an adult who reads a lot we found that there are no significant differences in number of books read between girls who do and do not live with adults who are keen readers. This was true whether the adult was male or female.

We also asked ourselves whether adults in a family appear to have an influence on the book choices which children make. We have already pointed out that there is an increasing amount of reading of what might be termed 'adult fiction' from ages 10 to 12 to 14. Apart from the obvious reasons to do with increasing maturity, we speculated that this pattern might have something to do with an interest in and ability to read the adult books which are available in the house, or which adults might be seen reading, or may have recommended. The interviews suggested that this was unlikely.

The 'adult' authors such as John Grisham, Virginia Andrews, Stephen King, and Michael Crichton are unlikely to have been chosen as a result of

Table 5.11 Adult family reading and girls' perceptions of the amount they read

	Perceives herself as reading a large amount	Perceives herself as reading quite a lot	Perceives herself as reading about an average amount	Perceives herself as reading not very much	Perceives herself as reading only a little
% girls living with no adults who reads a lot	16.7	27.8	32.0	17.0	6.5
% girls living with 1+ adult who reads a lot	18.6	30.4	33.4	13.3	4.3

adult recommendation since a substantial proportion of the girls and boys interviewed felt that families are unlikely to recommend good books. It was generally agreed that parents chose dull, boring, difficult and old-fashioned books. The common view was that parents had different tastes and would want you to read serious and/or educational books which they thought would 'do you good' but which did not usually appeal. Parents would recommend boring books also because they are simply not on the 'same wavelength' as their children.

These interview findings about family members recommendations were consistent across age groups and between both sexes:

> I think the ones that my family recommend to me are either for older children or, I don't know . . . but when they say 'why don't you read this one?' and it would be a big one and you know . . . I wouldn't really understand it. (Girl, 10)

> I have no idea why children would want to read books chosen by their family. (Boy, 10)

> Well if someone recommends it in your family, it depends, if it's like a parent you think, oh no they're going to be watching me, I'll have to read this book . . . like even if you don't enjoy it. Because like, books that parents usually recommend you don't enjoy them. You still read them but, well, like you jump a few pages every so often and then you just get a vague outline. And if they still ask you you just say, oh yeah, this has just happened and that happened. (Boy, 10)

My family recommends old books like *Treasure Island* which dad recommended. I don't really read books my family recommends. (Girl, 12)

My family are weird so I wouldn't read the books they read. (Girl, 12)

This is not to suggest that interviewees inevitably rejected books recommended by the adults in their families. Mothers fared rather better than fathers in this matter; most interviewees felt that mothers are more likely than fathers to offer reliable recommendations, and 14-year-old boys in particular were willing to accept adult recommendations, especially from their mothers.

If parents appear to be less important than might be supposed in influencing children's reading choices, is this also true of siblings? We considered whether there might be discernible influences upon the reading of children who live with other children who are keen readers. These findings are markedly different to those related to adult readers. Question 20 of the questionnaire asked respondents to identify brothers and sisters, or other children who might live with them. They were asked to identify the sex of the sibling and whether or not the child 'reads a lot'. Nearly half of the sample (46.1 per cent) reported living with a child who reads a lot. Roughly one-third (30 per cent) live with a girl who reads a lot; and one-fifth (21.4 per cent) live with a boy who reads a lot.

How does this relate to the children's perceptions of themselves as readers? Boys who live with another child who reads a lot do have a more positive view of themselves as readers than boys who do not (Table 5.12). They also see themselves as doing slightly more reading, and the figures on the numbers of books they read in the four weeks prior to the survey bear this out (Tables 5.13 and 5.14). The sex of the sibling who reads a lot is not relevant to this finding. There are no notable differences between the perceptions of boys who live with male or female siblings who read a lot in relation to their judgement of their own competence at reading, the amount of reading they do, nor indeed to the numbers of books they had read in the weeks before the survey.

The picture for girls is similar (Tables 5.15, 5.16 and 5.17). Girls who live with a sibling who reads a lot are slightly more likely to have a positive view of their reading abilities than girls who do not. They regard themselves as reading more than their counterparts who do not live with siblings who are keen readers, and the numbers of books they cite bear this out. Again, for girls, the sex of the sibling is not relevant to their perceptions of their reading abilities and the amounts of reading they do.

Although the questionnaire did not directly address questions to do with the influence of peers, it became very obvious during the interviews that friends play a very large part in the reading choices which children

Table 5.12 Sibling reading and boys' perceptions of their own reading abilities

	Perceives himself as a very good reader	Perceives himself as a good reader	Perceives himself as an average reader	Perceives himself as not a very good reader	Perceives himself as a poor reader
% boys living with no children who read a lot	18.8	35.2	34.3	9.3	2.3
% boys living with 1+ child who reads a lot	21.8	36.1	31.7	8.6	1.7

Table 5.13 Sibling reading and boys' perceptions of the amount they read

	Perceives himself as reading a large amount	Perceives himself as reading quite a lot	Perceives himself as reading about an average amount	Perceives himself as reading not very much	Perceives himself as reading only a little
% boys living with no child who read a lot	9.1	17.5	35.7	24.7	13.0
% boys living with 1+ child who reads a lot	11.0	22.1	37.1	21.0	8.8

make. Again this finding was consistent across age and sex groupings. The finding supports others which recognise the importance of the peer group in schooling. Robertson and Symons (1996), for example, have shown that pupils who come from socio-economically disadvantaged backgrounds, who are in schools where a high proportion of other pupils come from households with parents in professional and managerial occupations, tend to make significantly more progress than similar pupils in other schools – i.e. a peer group with high expectations and abilities raises the performance for all pupils.

It was certainly clear from the interview transcripts that peer culture is

Table 5.14 Sibling readers and boys' reading in the four weeks prior to the survey

	Read 0 books in last 4 weeks	Read 1–3 books in last 4 weeks	Read 4–6 books in last 4 weeks	Read 7+ books in last 4 weeks
% boys living with no child who reads a lot	29.6	52.6	13.7	4.1
% boys living with 1+ child who reads a lot	21.1	56.7	17.5	4.7

Table 5.15 Sibling reading and girls' perceptions of their own reading abilities

	Perceives herself as a very good reader	Perceives herself as a good reader	Perceives herself as an average reader	Perceives herself as not a very good reader	Perceives herself as a poor reader
% girls living with no child who read a lot	20.5	39.9	31.2	6.8	1.5
% girls living with 1+ child who reads a lot	24.2	41.2	27.2	5.9	1.5

a major influence on reading choices and habits. All the girls and most of the boys interviewed thought it likely that you would read books recommended by friends. It was generally believed that friends had much in common and would share the same taste in books. Boys in particular were clear that friends have the same taste and share the same interests and that therefore their judgements could be trusted. Friends were likely to recommend 'good, exciting books'; friends' judgements could be trusted and they 'wouldn't lie to you'.

It was also important to the interviewees that they were seen to be in tune with the peer culture by being able to talk about books currently fashionable amongst their group. Three girls expressed caution about friends' recommendations – one said she would always read the blurb

Table 5.16 Sibling readers and girls' perceptions of they amount they read

	Perceives herself as reading a large amount	Perceives herself as reading quite a lot	Perceives herself as reading about an average amount	Perceives herself as reading not very much	Perceives herself as reading only a little
% girls living with no child who read a lot	17.3	26.6	33.6	16.5	6.0
% girls living with 1+ child who reads a lot	18.9	32.9	32.1	12.2	3.9

Table 5.17 Sibling readers and girls' reading in the four weeks prior to the survey

	Read 0 books in last 4 weeks	Read 1–3 books in last 4 weeks	Read 4–6 books in last 4 weeks	Read 7+ books in last 4 weeks
% girls living with no child who reads a lot	18.7	51.9	21.9	7.5
% girls living with 1+ child who reads a lot	13.2	52.3	25.8	8.8

anyway, one would only consider recommendations from 'brainy' friends and the third would definitely not read books recommended to her by one particular friend – but the overwhelming opinion was that friends were a major source of influence on reading choices:

> Yes, my friend recommended 'The Waitress', that was good. So was Judy Blume. She likes the same sort of things as me and it's funny because we go 'oh that bit is good' together. (Girl, 10)

> My friends have recommended me some books and I've read them because they make them sound so exciting and also they say 'oh it's

brilliant' because it has all these magical things in it. I think that's what makes me read them with my friends. I think it's the way that they tell it to you or just explain it, like . . . or if they just say 'oh it's excellent and I've read it over and over again, I just can't stop reading it. (Girl, 10)

It's like oh, a friend said it's good so it must be . . . it's like . . . I don't know . . . you wouldn't read that book otherwise. It's like oh, so and so said it was good so let's just try it out because . . . you know . . . friends usually like . . . they've got the same taste in things, they like the same things, yes. (Boy, 10)

Friends spread the word about good or boring books. (Girl, 12)

Friends don't lie. Well, they don't spread round the bad things, they spread around the good points so you might think yeah. I wouldn't take it from one friend, it would have to be a couple of friends. (Girl, 12)

I wouldn't mind reading a book that one of my friends thought was good. If you think it's good or boring, you pass on the word and everyone gets a good read. (Boy, 12)

Well, if a book is recommended, like if a friend says it's good, then you normally want to find out. If they don't think it's very good, I just won't read it. (Boy, 14)

From a friend's point of view, if he has enjoyed it, he'll want you to enjoy it as we and from my point of view it's because I have an opinion on it. Like if my friends like it I'll have a go. It's like you have an opinion before you start reading it. (Boy, 14)

The findings reported here – that for both boys and girls the influence of having other children who read at home is more important than the influence of having adults who read a lot, taken with the interview phase finding that children are more influenced by peers in their reading choices than by adults – have direct implications for teachers and Family Literacy Projects. The findings suggest that the important emphasis which is often given to the parental role in encouraging children's reading should be supplemented by serious attention to encouraging collaborative reading activities with siblings and peers.

Reading and speakers of a language other than English

In the questionnaire respondents were asked whether they spoke a language other than English at home. Of these, 18.3 per cent responded positively. No question was asked about the particular language spoken although some children wrote in the name of a language, sometimes 'French'. It might well be that an proportion of this sample are secondary school pupils who considered that the modern foreign language they were learning at school allowed them to answer the question about speaking a second language positively. Nevertheless the correlation of positive answers to this question with self-report on ethnicity suggests that the question is not badly compromised by the 'school language' factor.

Of the total sample, 12.3 per cent of the children replied that they could write in a home language other than English. This constitutes 68 per cent of the group who said they could speak another language. Of the total sample, 12.6 per cent said they could read in this language, which constitutes 70.1 per cent of the group who said they could speak another language. More than one in ten of children in our survey therefore considered themselves literate in a language other than English.

The findings below refer to *speakers* of a language other than English (Table 5.18). Except where specifically mentioned the findings can also be said to relate to those who can read and write in another language since there was no significant difference in the findings for these groups.

In the *Children's Reading Choices* sample there was no association between any particular socio-economic group and those who identified themselves as speakers of a language other than English at home, and there is no significant difference in the answers given by boys and girls within this particular group.

Speakers of languages other than English are slightly more likely to read magazines, comics or newspapers than other respondents: more than eight out of ten regularly read periodicals (85 per cent, compared to 82 per cent for the sample as a whole). They had also read slightly more books than other respondents.

Finding reading material in the home language appears to be difficult however. Just 6.4 per cent of the sample, half of those children who can read a second language, found it easy to find materials they enjoy reading in this language.

Table 5.18 Speakers of a language other than English: numbers of books read

	Read 0 books in last 4 weeks	Read 1–3 books in last 4 weeks	Read 4–6 books in last 4 weeks	Read 7+ books in last 4 weeks
% speakers of a language other than English	17.5	54.5	19.9	8.0
% whole sample	20.6	53.4	19.5	6.2

When asked whether they had a favourite writer, or favourite series of books, this group within the sample were slightly more likely than others to answer positively. Across all three ages, 67 per cent did have favourite writers or series, (compared to a figure of 65 per cent for the whole sample). The figure for those who read (rather than speak) another language was, as one might expect, slightly higher with 70 per cent having a favourite.

In relation to the question about the amount of reading children perceived themselves as doing, the figures for speakers of a language other than English entirely match those for the sample as a whole (Table 5.19). These children's views of their own reading abilities are also consistent with the sample as a whole. Certainly the views this group of children have of themselves as readers are, as with the whole sample, very positive, with 90 per cent considering themselves to be average or better readers.

Table 5.19 Speakers of a language other than English: perceptions of their own reading abilities

	Very good	Good	Average	Not very good	Poor
% speakers of a language other than English	21.0	38.1	31.3	7.8	1.8
% of total sample	21.1	38.0	31.3	7.8	1.8

Table 5.20 Speakers of a language other than English: frequency of library borrowing

	Borrow weekly	Borrow fortnightly	Borrow about once a month	Borrow only sometimes
% speakers of a language other than English	22.1	12.2	17.4	32.7
% of total sample	8.2	14.1	14.6	34.4

Book borrowing from libraries by speakers of languages other than English is higher than in the sample as a whole (Table 5.20). More than eight out of ten children (84.4 per cent) said that they borrowed books from the public library, compared to 71.3 per cent in the whole sample.

Purchase of reading material is also high, and consistent with the sample as a whole. Eighty-nine per cent of the bilingual group said they had bought a book, comic, magazine or newspaper in the previous year, compared with 88 per cent of the whole sample.

In summary then, the findings are very positive in relation to children for whom English is an additional language. These children have very positive views of themselves as readers, read slightly more books and magazines than others, and use the library significantly more than others. However half of these children say that it is difficult to find reading material in their home language. Despite strenuous efforts on the part of some schools and LEAs , it is clear that there is a continuing need for publishers, libraries and schools to recognise languages other than English in the provision of reading material for this age group.

Summary

- There is a clear relationship between socio-economic background and the number of books children read.
- There are no significant differences between the amounts of reading that children of different ethnic groups are engaged in.
- There are notable differences between the favourite authors and favourite genres of children from different socio-economic groups, and, in some cases, between the periodicals they choose to read.
- There is little, if any, relationship between children taking a positive view of their own reading ability and living with adults who are keen readers.
- There is a significant positive relationship between children's enthusiasm for reading and the amount of reading they do, and living with a sibling who reads a lot.
- There is a significant positive relationship between the amount of reading children do, and living with a sibling who reads a lot.
- Book recommendations by friends and peers are more important to children than recommendations from adults. However, mothers' book recommendations are more likely to find favour than fathers'.

References

Gorman, T. and Fernandez, C. (1992), *Reading in Recession*, National Foundation for Educational Research, Slough

Robertson, D. and Symons, J. (1996), 'Do peer groups matter? Peer group versus schooling effects on academic attainment', Discussion Paper no. 311, London School of Economics

Robinson, P. (1997), *Literacy, Numeracy and Economic Performance*, Centre for Economic Performance, London

Chapter 6

Children's reading habits

In this chapter we consider information on children's reading habits: their use of public libraries, the places they choose to read, their ownership of books, and their purchasing habits. Since the *Children's Reading Choices* survey was concerned with children's voluntary reading we were interested in how children acquired the material they read. We asked about the frequency of public library borrowing, and about children's habits with regard to book and periodical purchase, including point of purchase. We also acquired information about children's perceptions of the numbers of books owned and available in the home, especially since there have been studies which suggest that there is a direct relation between reading ability and the number of books available in the home (Thorndike, 1973).

The purchase of books and periodicals

Children were asked 'Have you bought any books, comics, magazines, or newspapers this year?' Nearly nine out of ten children (88.1 per cent) answered positively. Table 6.1 lists shops and other purchase points mentioned in the survey by more than 1.0 per cent of the sample (3.0 per cent of the mentions were non-identifiable in terms of the categories given below). Respondents were given space to mention up to six shops.

  This relatively short list by no means gives an indication of the range of purchase points children used to buy books. Nearly fifty different locations were noted as places for book purchase including 'the off-licence', 'car boot sale', 'computer games shop', 'mail order', 'school shop', 'Topshop', and 'library sale'. The individual entries were aggregated according to types of shop, the calculation ignoring all figures below 0.25 per cent. Although, in a number of instances the identification of shop name with type is insecure (we were unable for instance to identify the type of shop 'Foggins' might be), it is very clear that most reading material which children of this age buy for themselves comes from local shops, either the newsagent or a local general store (Table 6.2).

Table 6.1 Percentage of total sample mentioning purchasing point

Purchasing point	%
Local newsagent	38.6
Local village or town store	25.8
W. H. Smith	25.3
Local bookshop	5.7
The Post Office	5.3
Fourboys	4.8
Tesco	4.4
Dillons	4.3
Martins newsagents	3.5
Sainsbury's	3.0
Asda	2.5
Spar	2.2
Waterstones	2.0
Station/airport/holiday shop	1.7
Woolworths	1.7
A kiosk	1.6
John Menzies	1.5
A garage	1.4
Circle K	1.2
Volume One	1.1

Table 6.2 Main purchase points for periodicals and books

Shop type	% of sample purchasing here
Newsagent	49.0
Local village/town general store	25.8
W. H. Smith	25.3
Supermarkets/grocery chains	16.8
Bookshops	12.3

Calculations were made relating to age, socio-economic group, ethnicity and sex for all shops/points of purchase that were mentioned by over 1.5 per cent of the sample. In some shops the balance in the use by different sexes is statistically significant. These are W. H. Smith, Tesco, Sainsbury's, Dillons, Waterstones, local bookshops, Asda, and Fourboys. In all these cases girls were the more likely customers. There are two sorts of shop here, supermarkets and bookshops. The figure relating to girls' more frequent purchasing of reading material from supermarkets might be explained in cultural/domestic terms (that is, that girls and women are more likely to be shopping in supermarkets for food and household supplies). The comparative reluctance of boys to purchase from bookshops is evident from the findings. The reason for this reluctance is unclear from the data.

The overall picture of shop use by age is complex. There is an obvious and significant increase in use of the major bookshops as children get older which can be explained in terms of increasing independence of children and the ability of older children to visit the town centres where major bookshops are usually located. But an increase also in the use of local newsagents and buying from kiosks as children get older suggests a more likely explanation has to do simply with the increased purchasing power of older children.

There are three areas of these findings for which it is difficult to find immediate explanations. First, although most outlets have significant differences in the ages of their child customers, some (namely, Sainsbury's, Asda, Martin's the newsagents, and the Post Office) do not. Second, there is an interesting phenomenon relating to purchase from local bookshops, local general stores and the newsagent Fourboys. In all three instances numbers of young people buying from these outlets significantly increases between age 10 and 12, but then significantly declines again. This is perhaps accounted for by a rise in pocket-money income between 10 and 12, and a greater propensity to shop further abroad by 14. Third, there are two cases where there are differences in the purchasing patterns of different ethnic groups. A significantly larger percentage of those who identified themselves as in groups other than 'white' mentioned buying reading material from W. H. Smith (26.3 per cent as against 18.7 per cent) and from the local village or town general stores (26.7 per cent as against 18.2 per cent).

Where statistical significance occurs in relation to socio-economic groups this is almost entirely to do with the small number of outlets which are patronised often by young people from social groups A and B and much less by members of other social groups. These outlets are Waterstones and 'local bookshops'. Perhaps, if one considers the different sort of reading material on offer in the different outlets, it ought to be a cause for concern that specialist bookshops, rather than general stores which sell books, such as W. H. Smith, are not used by children other than those in the most advantaged social groups. One might guess that this is the result of the different purchasing power of the different groups, with bookshops being perceived by those in lower socio-economic groups as expensive. Information from the interviews suggests that the explanation is also partly to do with the intimidating number of books available in a bookshop with children not knowing where to go to find what they want. Obviously some children are more confident in bookshops than others. However, all but one interviewee saw it as difficult to find and choose books in these shops.

> Yes I buy some books. It's not that easy to find them in shops . . . I get confused because sometimes they just put the letter of the author and I can't always remember their name. (Girl, 12)

> Sometimes if you don't really know, it's a bit hard to choose. (Girl, 12)

> It can be difficult, a lot of the books I like are in pretty weird places. I think they need to know where books are a lot better, you don't know where they are and you have to ask someone to show you and half the time they don't know. (Boy, 14)

The list of suggestions which children of all ages offered for improving bookshops suggests that the major reason for the low numbers of children who purchase books in specialist shops is their perception that these shops are not 'user-friendly' for children. Some interviewees suggested arranging books by author, others preferred organisation on shelves by type and content. Some chose to categorise by sex and others by age and levels of difficulty. One-third of all those interviewed suggested more posters and advertising. Others proposed better signs. It was felt that books should be cheaper and that there should be a chance to sample books by reading extracts in catalogues. Several said that the assistants should be more helpful and encourage children to look through books. It was suggested that children are just rushed through and that it would be better if a special area was set aside. Books should be advertised more and there should be special promotions like a 'Book of the Week'. It was generally felt that bookshops could be livened up and ought to become more colourful, that summary sheets of books could be provided, that there could be more pictures and that surveys should be carried out to find out what children really like:

> At the newspaper shop where I go they've just got a new selection of Point Horror books. If I were the manager of W. H. Smith I'd put more books in the shops and I'd make them more exciting. I'd put a special kiddies section on for pocket money price because not many kids get loads of pocket money so I think I'd put them down in price as well. Little kids' books are expensive. (Girl, 10)

> Well I'd put funny books in certain sections and like it'd be like other books, adultish books on one side and comics next to the funny books. So the kids like, they've got their little space so next time they come in they don't have to like go 'I want this book by such and such' or have to search through the whole place. (Boy, 10)

> I'd put more signs up and show people where the books were. I'd put the authors down and advertise them more. (Girl, 12)

> I'd make it a comfortable place, like in a corner where people don't walk through or feel rushed. (Girl, 12)

Make children aware of how reading helps you later on in life, get the point across. I don't know really, posters and just something that'll stand out (Boy, 14)

I would probably put them all out on a board and put all the characters together like a library. (Boy, 10)

None of these suggestions however would be likely to please one 10-year-old boy whose view was:

Book buying? It's a waste of money because you only read them once. (Boy, 10)

Purchasing patterns

Responses to the survey question asking children to tell us whether they had bought a book, a comic, a magazine, or a newspaper 'this year' suggest that in relation to the total sample the most commonly purchased item was a magazine, followed by a book, newspaper, and then comic. Over half of all children had bought a book for themselves in the last year; the 10-year-old quoted above who thought book buying was a waste of money was very much in the minority.

When purchasing figures are analysed in terms of socio-economic group very obvious patterns emerge. Book and magazine buying is highest in social group A. It is lowest in social group D/E. However this pattern does not occur in relation to the purchase of comics and newspapers. Here there is a stronger purchasing habit in the less advantaged social groups, demonstrated by the figures in Table 6.3.

These figures suggest that purchasing patterns are limited primarily by income levels: more members of social groups D/E than members of social group A are buying the cheaper items, i.e. comics and newspapers. Other data indicate that far fewer members of social groups D/E than social group A bought two or more of the most expensive of these three items, i.e. a magazine.

Table 6.3 Percentage purchase of magazine, comics and newspapers in the survey year by socio-economic group

Social group	Magazine	Comic	Newspaper
A	81.6	26.2	28.4
B	83.5	29.6	37.1
C_1	82	29.8	36.7
C_2	79.3	29.8	40.9
D/E	79.5	33.3	42.2

Table 6.4 Purchase of books, magazines, comics and newspapers in the survey year by sex

No. of items	% Boys	% Girls
I book	31.6	36.3
2+ books	10.5	15.4
I magazine	53.4	50.6
2+ magazines	22.1	33.9
I comic	36.0	15.0
2+ comics	6.0	4.0
I newspaper	37.3	27.3
2+ newspapers	7.4	5.4

Table 6.5 Purchase of books, magazines, comics and newspapers in the survey year by age

No. of items	% 10+	% 12+	% 14+
I book	35.9	32.6	31.8
2+ books	12.1	13.3	14.1
I comic	34.2	24.5	1.6
2+ comics	6.0	5.2	2.8
I magazine	51.3	54.4	51.1
2+ magazines	19.9	32.3	39.1
I newspaper	27.5	35.2	38.1
2+ newspapers	4.6	7.7	8.1

Table 6.6 Purchase of magazines and newspapers in the survey year by ethnicity

No. of items	% 'White'	% Other groups
0 magazines	19.0	28.9
I magazine	52.1	51.4
2+ magazines	28.5	19.7
0 newspapers	62.0	53.5
I newspaper	31.7	39.1
2+ newspapers	6.3	7.4

The figures relating to sex also offer clear patterns, as shown in Table 6.4. Girls are more likely to buy books and magazines than boys. Boys are more likely to buy comics and newspapers than girls. The pattern of book buying is similar in each age group, but this is not the case with newspapers, comics and magazines. Purchase of comics decreases dramatically after age 12, while purchase of newspapers and magazines increases (see Table 6.5).

There was no significant difference between different ethnic groups in relation to the purchase of books or comics (Table 6.6). However, the percentage of those identifying themselves as 'white' who buy magazines is significantly higher than that of those who identify themselves as being in other ethnic groups. Also, the percentage of those identifying themselves as 'white' who buy newspapers is significantly lower than those identifying themselves as belonging to other groups.

Children's ownership of books

Children were asked: 'Do you own any books yourself?' If their answer was positive they were then asked about the number they owned (see Table 6.7). The questionnaire allowed the children to respond within six categories. All 7,976 children responded to the first part of the question. 95.7 per cent reported owning their own books. Nearly 40 per cent of children report owning over fifty books and over 60 per cent say they own twenty-six books or more.

Almost all pupils from social group A claim personal book ownership (99.1 per cent) (see Table 6.8). The figures reduce slightly for each subsequent social group, a pattern that may be as much the result of economic as cultural circumstances, since the findings on magazine and newspaper purchase suggest that there is no particular reluctance on the part of any social group to buying reading material.

Across the age categories there is an equivalence in the percentage of children who say they own books (Table 6.9). At the age of 10, 96.5 per cent of children say they own books. This figure drops slightly by the age of 12 to 95.8 per cent and very slightly again to 95.2 per cent by 14 years. However, older pupils report owning smaller numbers of books (Table 6.9). Almost half of 10-year-olds claim ownership of more than fifty books. This is true for only 36.7 per cent of 12-year-olds, and under 30 per cent of 14-year-olds. Less than 10 per cent of 10-year-olds say they own ten or fewer books whereas more than twice this percentage of 14-year-olds claim ten or fewer books in their personal ownership. It is difficult to know whether this trend reflects actual ownership; however, it is clear

Table 6.7 Children's perceptions of the number of books they own

Books owned	% of total sample
None	4.3
1–9	15.7
10–25	18.3
26–50	23.0
51–100	22.6
100+	16.3

Table 6.8 Perceptions of book ownership by % socio-economic group

Social group	10 or fewer	11–25	26–50	51–100	100+
A	7.7	12.8	26.8	32.7	19.9
B	7.3	15.6	25.0	28.0	24.2
C_1	13.7	19.6	25.8	24.4	16.5
C_2	20.3	20.9	23.1	20.1	15.6
D/E	26.9	19.1	23.4	19.41	11.3
U	19.8	20.0	22.4	22.6	15.2

Table 6.9 Perceptions of book ownership by % age

Age group	10 or fewer	11–25	26–50	51–100	100+
10+	10.0	14.1	24.8	28.7	22.4
12+	17.8	20.7	23.3	22.7	15.6
14+	22.3	23.2	23.7	18.8	12.1

Table 6.10 Perceptions of book ownership by % sex

Sex	10 or fewer	11–25	26–50	51–100	100+
Boys	18.8	19.1	22.9	21.7	17.5
Girls	13.8	19.1	25.1	25.6	16.4

Table 6.11 Perceptions of book ownership by % ethnic group

Group	10 or fewer	11–25	26–50	51–100	100+
'White'	15.1	18.8	24.3	24.2	17.6
Other groups	26.0	20.9	21.9	19.1	12.2

that children's perceptions of book ownership change with age. The trend here accords with Whitehead's findings in the 1970s. Initially it might appear a surprising finding. It might be explained though by the fact that whereas younger children perceive their books as belonging exclusively to them, their personal property, older children see their books as jointly owned, part of the family stock.

If we consider perceptions of book ownership by sex then slightly more girls (97.4 per cent) than boys (94.5 per cent) report owning their own books (see Table 6.10). Girls also see themselves as owning a larger number; 67 per cent of girls and 62 per cent of boys claim ownership of 26 books or more.

A larger percentage of children identifying themselves as 'white' (96.6 per cent) claim book ownership than children who identify themselves in other groups (90.1 per cent) (Table 6.11). This is true also for the number of books children in the different groups say they own. It may be that the difficulty in acquiring books in their mother tongue that is experienced by children who speak English as a second language accounts in some part for these figures.

Book ownership and reading

As one would expect there is a positive relationship between the number of books children claim to own and the amount of reading they say they do. Also as might be expected children who say they own a large number of books were more likely to have read a book in the four weeks prior to the survey.

Almost three-quarters of children (74.4 per cent) who said they read about an average amount or more also own books. Of those who claim ownership of 100+ books a third also say they read a large amount. A further 29.4 per cent say they read quite a lot. Of those children who say they own over 50 books, 87.9 per cent had also read a book in the last four weeks. However, of those who claim they own 10 or fewer books, only 3.7 per cent say they read a large amount and 14.4 per cent say they read quite a lot. Almost half of the group owning 10 or fewer books thought they read a below average amount. Of those children who do not own books, 60 per cent thought they read 'not very much' or 'only a little'. One in five (20.1 per cent) children who claim to own some books report reading no books in the previous month. However, this figure rises to 43.7 per cent for those children who say they do not own any books.

Children who own books are more likely to think they are good at reading than children who do not own books, and children who own a large number of books are more likely to think they are good at reading than those who own small numbers of books. Sixty per cent of those who owned books also thought they were 'good' or 'very good' at reading. Of those who did not own books, 59 per cent thought they were average or below average at reading. Of those children who own 100+ books, almost three-quarters (74.5 per cent), also thought they were 'good' or 'very good' at reading. However, of those children who claimed they owned 10 or fewer books, over half (53.8 per cent) thought they were average or below at reading.

Public library borrowing

Children were asked in the questionnaire: 'Do you borrow books from the public library?' If their answer was positive, they were then asked about the frequency of their borrowing habits. All participants responded to this question. Seven out of ten children in the survey (71.3 per cent) say they do borrow public library books, but as Table 6.12 shows this borrowing is regular for only a minority of children.

Table 6.12 Frequency of book borrowing from public libraries

Frequency	% of total sample
About once a week	8.2
About every two weeks	14.1
About once a month	14.6
Only sometimes	34.4
Never	28.7

Just as book purchase from local bookshops, local general stores and newsagents increases between age 10 and 12, but then declines again, so it is with public library borrowing (see Table 6.13). Three-quarters of 12-year-old children claim to borrow books from the public library. The figure is slightly lower for 10-year-olds, and slightly lower again for 14-year-olds.

In general though as children get older they borrow library books less frequently. Ten-year-old children are three times more likely to borrow books on a weekly basis than 14-year-old children. Over half of all 14-year-old children say they borrow books 'only sometimes'.

Table 6.13 Frequency of book borrowing by % age

Age	Once a week	Every 2 weeks	Once a month	Only sometimes	Never
10+	15.0	22.1	17.3	39.9	5.8
12+	11.3	19.7	20.1	43.6	5.3
14+	5.1	13.1	20.6	52.6	8.6

Table 6.14 Frequency of book borrowing by % sex

Sex	Once a week	Every 2 weeks	Once a month	Only sometimes	Never
Boys	7.8	11.9	13.0	34.1	33.1
Girls	8.5	16.4	16.4	34.8	23.9

As all the other findings might lead us to expect, girls say they borrow more library books than boys do and that they borrow books more frequently (Table 6.14). Of the 28 per cent of children who say they never borrow books, the larger percentage is boys. Of girls, 41.3 per cent say they borrow books at least monthly, whereas this is true for only 32.7 per cent of boys.

The findings relating socio-economic grouping and library borrowing also match other patterns (Table 6.15). The overall trend is for children from the more advantaged social groups to report making greater use of public libraries than others do. The largest percentage of children who say they borrow library books are from social group A and there is a steady decline in borrowing as we move down the social scale.

Table 6.15 Book borrowing by socio-economic group

Social group	% using library
A	79.9
B	76.3
C_1	72.0
C_2	70.6
D/E	65.4

There is also a trend for children from the more advantaged socio-economic groups to report more frequent book borrowing (Table 6.16). However, it is particularly notable that the children who say they borrow books the most frequently, that is, on a weekly basis, come from socio-economic groups C_2 and D/E.

Table 6.16 Frequency of book borrowing by % socio-economic group

Social group	Once a week	Every 2 weeks	Once a month	Only sometimes	Never
A	5.9	15.6	17.7	41.0	19.8
B	5.9	16.2	17.6	36.7	23.5
C_1	6.9	13.5	15.6	36.1	27.9
C_2	8.9	14.0	14.5	33.6	29.0
D/E	10.2	9.3	13.1	32.8	34.6

Table 6.17 Frequency of book borrowing by % ethnicity

	Once a week	Every 2 weeks	Once a month	Only sometimes	Never
'White'	7.5	13.9	14.6	35.1	28.9
Other	13.4	15.3	14.3	30.0	27.0

The findings relating to ethnicity reveal that there are no significant difference between the different groups in terms of use of the public library to borrow books (Table 6.17). However, children identifying themselves as 'white' borrow books less frequently than those who identify themselves in other groups.

Ironically children are more likely to borrow books from the public library if they own books themselves. Nearly three-quarters of those who own books are also library users. Of those who do not own books, 57.4 per cent do not visit public libraries. There is also a positive relationship between the number of books children say they own and borrowing from the public library. Nearly eight out of ten children (78.4 per cent) who say they own 100+ books also say they borrow library books, whereas just under six out of ten children (58.7 per cent) who own ten or fewer books say they borrow from public libraries.

Libraries do not therefore necessarily act as a substitute source of reading material for those children with few books. In fact, children tend to borrow books more frequently from a public library the more books they own. Almost half (47.8 per cent) of those pupils who claim they own 100+ books also say they borrow library books at least once a month. Less than one third (27.5 per cent) of those children who own 10 or fewer books borrow from the public library at least once a month.

These figures suggest that a virtuous circle exists. Children who own books, think of themselves as good readers, read a lot, and frequently borrow books from libraries – though where this circle starts is a matter for conjecture. Conversely, many of those who do not think of themselves as good readers, own few books, read less than others and visit the library less often than others. This is a phenomenon recognised in the research literature on children's reading development as 'The Matthew Principle' (Stanovitch, 1986) after the parable of the talents in the St Matthew's Gospel – 'to those that have shall be given; from those that have not shall be taken away even that which they have'.

Summary

- Children buy their reading material from a very wide range of sources.
- Most reading material bought by 10–14-year-olds comes from local shops, particularly newsagents and general stores.
- Purchasing points and patterns differ according to the sex, age and socio-economic background of the child.
- The overwhelming majority of children report owning books. Nearly 40 per cent of children report owning over 50 books.
- Children consider that they own fewer books as they grow older. There are also significant differences in book ownership in relation to sex, ethnicity and social class.

- There is a positive relationship between book ownership, the amount of reading children do and children's views of themselves as readers.
- As children grow older, they tend to borrow library books less frequently.
- Children from more advantaged socio-economic groups report borrowing more frequently from libraries than children from less advantaged groups.
- Children are more likely to borrow books from the public library if they own books themselves.

References

Stanovitch, K. (1986) 'Matthew Effects in Reading: some consequences of individual differences in the acquisition of literacy', *Reading Research Quarterly*, 21, pp. 360–407

Thorndike, R. L. (1973) *Reading Comprehension Education in Fifteen Countries*, USA: IEA

Chapter 7

Television viewing, computer use and reading

In this chapter we consider television viewing, computer use and reading on the evening prior to the survey. We consider the relationship between children's use of their leisure time for these different activities, and relate the survey findings to the age and sex of the children surveyed. We report briefly some of the interview findings on gender, computer use and reading. The Endpiece raises points about attitudes to the relationship between literacy and the different media.

Television viewing

There is still, and has been almost since the invention of television, a concern that television viewing detracts from a culture of literacy and, in particular, restricts the amount of reading children do. The image of television dominating lives at the expense of other activities recurs frequently in press reports. As long ago as 1955, when only one television channel was available in Britain, the BBC, with the Nuffield Foundation, sponsored an empirical study of the effect of television on the young (Himmelweit, 1958) the report of which contains sections entitled 'Reactions to Conflict, Crime and Violence on Television', 'Effects on Knowledge and School Performance' and 'Effects on Leisure and Interests'. One chapter considers the effects of television on reading and starts 'Many thoughtful people today are anxious about the effect of television on children's reading' (p. 32).

In England in the 1980s 98 per cent of homes possessed at least one television set (Gunter and McAleer, 1990) and that percentage is likely to have increased in the last ten years. The arrival of the personal computer and adult assumptions made about the time that children devote to playing computer games have increased anxieties about the potentially deleterious effects of screen viewing on reading habits. For example, in P. D. James' review of *A History of Reading* by Alberto Manguel (*Sunday Times* 28.6.96) she says: 'It seems evident that children, in particular, are reading less . . .' and links this misapprehension to the 'problem' of television viewing.

Clearly, the concern is not unreasonable since time spent watching television or playing computer games is not time devoted to reading. Many homes now possess not just one, but two, three or four televisions, and often a range of accessories such as video recorders, remote controls, and games consuls which encourage additional use of the screen. Time is a limited commodity. Television uses up time. If people spend more time watching television they must be spending less time doing something else. So is reading displaced when children spend time watching television?

It is important of course to attempt to gather data about the actual amounts of time children spend watching television if we wish to draw conclusions about the effect of television on time spent reading. Are children spending long hours slumped in front of various screens? Gunter and McAleer (1990) quote official viewing figures published by Broadcasters Audience Research Board (BARB). Their research suggests that the average daily amount of viewing done by children between 4 and 11 years old is between two and a half to three hours. It is worth noting from the BARB figures that, although many consider that children spend far too much time watching television, they are by no means the heaviest viewers. The BARB research suggests that every adult age group (except 16–24 years olds) exhibits a greater average number of hours per day watching television than children do. And it is worth speculating on how many adults read an average of 2.52 books per month as children in the *Children's Reading Choices* sample do.

In fact the children in our survey watch roughly equivalent amounts of television to those in the BARB sample. In the survey children were asked 'Did you watch television last night?' (see Table 7.1). If their answer was positive, they were then asked to specify how much time they spent on this activity. All respondents completed this question. Nearly all (95.2 per cent) had watched television on the previous evening. The majority (56.7 per cent) reported that they had viewed for 2½ hours or less, but over a quarter claimed to have watched television for more than 3½ hours.

Table 7.1 Amount of television viewing reported in one evening

Amount of viewing	% of total sample
None	4.8
Less than ½ hour	6.7
Between ½ and 1½ hours	22.4
Between 1½ and 2½ hours	22.8
Between 2½ and 3½ hours	17.1
More than 3½ hours	26.2

This table can usefully be set alongside figures which offer an indication of the amount of reading which children claimed to have done in the evening prior to the survey (see Chapter 1, Table 1.13) Two-thirds of the sample (65 per cent) reported doing some reading during the previous evening, but children generally reported spending significantly more time watching television than reading.

A critical question is whether 'heavy' television viewers spend less time reading than 'light' viewers do. Early research in America (Brown *et al.*, 1974; Robinson, 1969) indicated that children and teenagers soon learned how to accommodate large amounts of television viewing without sacrificing other activities. We examined the amount of children's reading in relation to the amount of television they claim to watch in one evening. Respondents were categorised in terms of the number of books they had read during the four-week period prior to the survey.

It can be seen from Table 7.2 that heavy readers are more likely than others to have watched no television on the evening prior to the survey. Those children who had read no books in the previous four weeks had watched the most television (more than 3½ hours). However, although there is a trend for children who are reading the most heavily to claim to have watched least television, it is also the case that nearly 20 per cent of those children who had read 7+ books over a four-week period, also claim to have watched more than 3½ hours of television in the evening prior to the survey. Whitehead's 1971 survey found an inverse relationship between the amount of television viewing and the amount of book reading in his sample, and this is generally true of the *Children's Reading*

Table 7.2 Amount of television viewing reported in one evening by % reader type categories

Reader type	No time	Less than 0.5 hours	0.5–1.5 hours	1.5–2.5 hours	2.5–3.5 hours	More than 3.5 hours
0 books	4.3	4.6	18.7	22.3	17.3	32.5
1–3 books	4.3	6.6	23.3	22.6	17.2	26.1
4–6 books	5.3	3.1	23.4	24.9	16.7	21.5
7+ books	7.6	10.0	24.6	20.6	17.4	19.6

Table 7.3 Amount of television viewing reported in one evening by % age

Age	No time	Less than 0.5 hours	0.5–1.5 hours	1.5–2.5 hours	2.5–3.5 hours	More than 3.5 hours
10+	5.8	3.8	21.6	20.7	17.6	25.6
12+	3.1	5.9	21.5	22.6	16.6	30.2
14+	4.9	4.9	24.4	25.7	17.2	23.0

Choices data. However, the relationship between reading and television viewing is not a simple one, as the American studies and Himmelweit's work demonstrate: some children manage to accommodate a considerable amount of television viewing and a considerable amount of reading in their leisure time activities.

The BARB figures suggest that viewing rises from 4 to 11 and drops off until it is at its lowest during late teens. Whitehead noted a steady decrease in viewing as age increases. The *Children's Reading Choices* survey findings are that the children who report watching the most television are in the 12-year-old category where 30 per cent claim to have watched television for at least 3½ hours the previous evening. By comparison, only about a quarter of children in the 10- and 14-year-old categories report this amount of viewing. (See Table 7.3.) It should also be noted that some children claim to watch television and read at the same time, as the interview data made clear. This reading was rarely concentrated book reading, as might be expected, but both boys and girls mentioned reading magazines and newspapers in front of the television.

Younger children were more likely to report reading during the evening prior to the survey, and they were more likely to report having read for longer periods of time (see Chapter 1, Table 1.15).

The amount of reading children do in an evening decreases with age. Of those children who said that they had not read at all, the largest percentage was of 14 year olds. Of 10-year-old children, 12.2 per cent reported that they had read for at least one and a half hours in the previous evening, whereas this figure is 10.4 per cent for 12-year-olds, and is 6.7 per cent for 14-year-olds.

Boys claim to watch television for longer periods of time than girls do: of those children who say they spend 3½ hours or more watching television, 30 per cent are boys as opposed to 22.1 per cent of girls (Table 7.4). Boys also report reading for less time in the evening than girls (Table 7.5). Seven out of ten girls report reading in the evening prior to the survey compared with six out of ten boys. Also, more girls say they had read for longer periods of time than boys. However there is no significant difference between the sexes for those children who report large amounts of reading (i.e. at least 2½ hours).

One of the conclusions of the Himmelweit study was that 'The less intelligent children and those from working-class homes do not read much even without television.' (p. 335). The *Children's Reading Choices* study does not consider the notion of intelligence in relation to reading habits, but it is obvious from our survey that socio-economic background is related to time spent reading or watching television (see Table 7.6). Children from higher socio-economic groups spend less time watching television than others. Almost one-third of children from groups C_2 and D/E report spending 3½ hours or more watching television. By

Table 7.4 Amount of television viewing reported in one evening by % sex

Sex	No time	Less than 0.5 hours	0.5–1.5 hours	1.5–2.5 hours	2.5–3.5 hours	More than 3.5 hours
Boys	5.0	6.3	20.4	21.3	16.9	30.0
Girls	4.2	7.0	24.8	24.5	17.4	22.1

Table 7.5 Amount of reading reported in one evening by % sex

Sex	No time	Less than 0.5 hours	0.5–1.5 hours	1.5–2.5 hours	2.5–3.5 hours	More than 3.5 hours
Boys	40.0	26.5	24.4	5.7	2.1	1.3
Girls	29.5	26.4	33.3	6.6	2.6	1.5

Table 7.6 Amount of television viewing reported in one evening by % socio-economic group

Social group	No time	Less than 0.5 hours	0.5–1.5 hours	1.5–2.5 hours	2.5–3.5 hours	More than 3.5 hours
A	6.5	7.7	28.0	23.0	20.1	14.7
B	4.8	3.6	29.4	24.3	16.0	16.8
C_1	4.4	5.5	22.9	24.4	19.1	23.6
C_2	3.9	5.0	20.4	22.8	16.5	31.4
D/E	4.1	6.1	18.6	20.6	18.9	31.7
U	5.4	7.7	20.1	21.4	16.1	29.3

Table 7.7 Amount of reading reported in one evening by % socio-economic group

Social group	No time	Less than 0.5 hours	0.5–1.5 hours	1.5–2.5 hours	2.5–3.5 hours	More than 3.5 hours
A	26.3	25.7	33.6	10.6	2.1	1.8
B	31.0	24.0	33.5	7.0	2.6	1.9
C_1	33.9	26.5	30.7	5.5	2.1	1.3
C_2	36.8	28.7	25.8	5.9	1.9	0.9
D/E	39.8	26.5	25.6	4.4	2.6	1.2

comparison, half as many children from socioeconomic group A claim the same amount.

There is a marked increase in the percentages of children in the less advantaged socio-economic group who reported not reading in the evening prior to the survey (see Table 7.7). However, amongst those children who claim to have read the most (more than two and a half hours), there is a notable similarity of response across all social groups. In both the data on television viewing and the data on one evening's reading there are no significant differences related to the children's ethnicity.

Reading and computer use

A great deal has been written about the effect of television on children's reading (for example, most recently, Robinson, 1997). There is much less written about the effect of computer use on children's reading, but we were aware when we constructed the questionnaire that both parents and teachers quite commonly voiced concerns about the nature of children's computer use, the amounts of time they devoted to it and the effects this had on children's reading development.

We therefore included the following question in the survey: 'Did you use a computer, or play any computer games last night?' If the answer was positive the child was then asked to specify how much time had been spent on this activity. We were deliberately unspecific about the nature of the computer use, simply wanting an indication of time spent on the computer. We had no doubts about the educational value of many computer games and saw no point in making hard and fast distinctions between games use and other computer uses. The issue seemed to us to be closely related to the television viewing one: that is, the amount of time that children had to spend on leisure-time reading, rather than the intrinsic merits of one medium over another. Interestingly, though, when asked about patterns of computer use during the interview phase of the project, most girls and all of the boys who commented on it assumed that boys' use of the computer was for playing fighting games and that girls were more likely to be using computers for word-processing purposes.

> They're into more games on computers. Some girls like them, I like computers. I think they use them for writing and things like that. (Girl, 10)

> I've got one but I hardly ever get to go on it because my brother is always on it. They probably think that computer games are more for boys though. It's usually things like fighting and football. (Girl, 10)

Nearly half of the sample (44.5 per cent) said they had used a computer on the evening prior to the survey (Table 7.8). Of those who responded positively the vast majority (72 per cent), reported that they had used the computer for one and a half hours or less. More 12-year-old children than any other age group reported using a computer during the evening before the questionnaire was completed. Computer use was lowest amongst 14-

Table 7.8 Amount of computer use reported in one evening by % age

Age	No time	Less than 0.5 hours	0.5–1.5 hours	1.5–2.5 hours	2.5–3.5 hours	More than 3.5 hours
10+	54.1	16.2	16.6	6.1	3.5	3.6
12+	52.5	16.1	18.6	6.4	3.1	3.2
14+	59.3	13.7	15.9	6.1	2.0	2.9

Table 7.9 Amount of computer use reported in one evening by % sex

Sex	No time	Less than 0.5 hours	0.5–1.5 hours	1.5–2.5 hours	2.5–3.5 hours	More than 3.5 hours
Boys	41.1	15.8	22.9	10.2	4.5	5.6
Girls	70.3	14.9	10.7	2.0	1.2	0.8

year-olds. There was a slight tendency for younger children to use a computer for longer periods of time.

Approximately twice as many boys as girls reported using a computer during the evening in question (58.6 per cent boys compared to 29.4 per cent girls) (Table 7.9). Boys also claimed to spend longer periods of time using the computer. One in ten boys (10.1 per cent) claimed to have spent at least 2½ hours at the computer, whereas this figure for girls was 2 per cent.

The *Children's Reading Choices* findings do not significantly link use of the computer with socio-economic group or ethnicity. Similar percentages of children from all social groups reported using a computer, although there was a relationship between the time children claimed to spend at the computer and socio-ecomonic group (see Table 7.10). Children from the less advantaged social groups spent more time using computers. Almost 5 per cent of children from social group D/E reported using a computer for more than three and a half hours; for social groups A , B and C_1 less than half this number report similar amounts of use.

Most importantly, there was no significant relationship between children's reported use of a computer and whether or not they had been reading that evening (Table 7.11). Similarly, there was no significant relationship between the amount of time children spent in computer use and the amount of time they spent reading during the four weeks prior to the survey, or the number of books they reported reading (Table 7.12). The findings here do not, therefore, suggest that using a computer has any notably adverse effects upon children's reading.

During the interview phase, although some girls expressed the view that computers have a positive impact upon reading, and made reference

Table 7.10 Amount of computer use reported in one evening by % socio-economic group

Social group	No time	Less than 0.5 hours	0.5–1.5 hours	1.5–2.5 hours	2.5–3.5 hours	More than 3.5 hours
A	54.0	20.4	16.8	5.0	1.8	2.1
B	57.4	18.0	16.0	4.6	2.3	1.7
C_1	55.2	16.9	17.8	5.8	2.6	1.7
C_2	54.7	14.9	16.3	6.9	3.0	4.2
D/E	50.9	13.7	18.3	7.0	5.5	4.7

Table 7.11 Association between amount of computer use reported and amount of reading reported in the previous evening

	Time spent on computer					
Time reported reading	No time	Less than 0.5 hours	0.5–1.5 hours	1.5–2.5 hours	2.5–3.5 hours	More than 3.5 hours
No time	56.3	12.7	17.4	7.3	3.1	3.2
Up to 0.5 hours	54.9	15.0	17.5	6.0	2.9	3.8
0.5–1.5 hours	55.7	18.2	16.4	5.2	2.3	2.1
1.5–2.5 hours	52.4	17.2	16.6	5.3	4.3	4.3
2.5–3.5 hours	46.5	21.1	16.2	4.9	4.9	6.5
More than 3.5 hours	50.9	15.5	10.9	3.2	1.8	12.7

Table 7.12 Association between amount of computer use and amount of reading reported over a four-week period

	Time spent on computer					
Number of books read	No time	Less than 0.5 hours	0.5–1.5 hours	1.5–2.5 hours	2.5–3.5 hours	More than 3.5 hours
0	53.6	12.1	17.8	3.1	3.7	4.7
1–3	55.8	15.2	17.4	5.9	2.7	3.1
4–6	55.1	17.8	16.5	5.2	2.8	2.6
7+	55.9	20.8	11.8	5.8	2.4	3.2

to the spell check and dictionary facilities, most girls were of the opinion that computer use has an adverse impact on reading – that you get 'wrapped up' in computers, distracting you from your reading. They argued that because computers are more obviously interactive than books, the tendency was to spend more time on them and to come to depend on them, to the detriment of reading. Boys on the other hand, took the view that computer use has a positive impact on reading because you have to read instructions carefully, read text in information programmes, and because of the benefits of word processing.

> Because, like on some computer games, it's got a lot of reading in it and you like . . . and you'll probably ask your mum what does that say and you'll probably see it in the book and you'll say oh yes, my mum told me what that said and you can read it without asking anyone. (Boy, 10)

> If you're playing games, then that is time that could be spent reading, but if you're typing up and you go back two or three pages and you go over it, you start reading, well that's probably better than playing a game. In a game you're using a joystick but if you're typing up then you're concentrating and you're reading over it so you can improve your reading skills as well. (Boy, 14)

Both girls and boys at these ages recognised the influence of computer games on boys, and most boys assumed that girls did not like computers, commenting for example that 'they weren't so good with the buttons'. All the girls spoken to, and most boys, agreed that boys are more interested and accomplished in the use of the computer and more willing to learn how to use it fully. Both girls and boys spoke of the possibility of boys becoming 'addicted' to computer games:

> Well, I suppose with boys, say if they are a computer freak yeah? and then say their best friend is a computer freak . . . you see all these games, a lot of them they're . . . like Streetfighter II or fighting games or maybe ones where you just have to shoot people . . . I like Street-fighter, it's great fun but boys are always trying to pretend they're so good at fighting but they're not because I've beaten boys so many times. They just do it because they think they're cool and then you just get addicted to it don't you? (Girl, 10)

> Boys play computer games, cos they're like into like gory things and like shooting and all that quickness and reactions and like everything, like on the Terminator, you've got your joy stick and you have to move it about and shoot him and things. Girls do writing, stories and

all that, like copying out of books and writing stories and making their own up, writing poems and stuff. (Boy, 10)

Yes, well boys like computers, well girls do as well still, but we sort of whenever there are computers, we sort of go over and have a look. (Boy, 10)

Boys are better at computers than girls. Girls are into all stuff like Barbie dolls and stuff and boys are just always on computers and mechanical things so they know more about computers than girls, football games . . . racing games. (Boy, 10)

Boys think computer games and football are more important than anything else . . . all combat games and fighting, I don't like them. Girls prefer their friends and listening to music and reading. There's no computer software for girls. (Girl, 12)

Boys are more lazy, boys would rather watch things in front of a screen rather than picture it in their mind, they're too lazy I think. A lot of girls like computers but they're not as crazed about it as boys. It's mainly fighting games isn't it, or soccer or something. (Girl, 14)

Oh, I'm not saying for everyone but most boys because they like fighting, violence, they like computer games and stuff. It's something for them to do, that they're interested in and that girls, well, are going out with their friends, having a gossip. It's just something like that they're interested in. (Girl, 14)

Summary

- The overwhelming majority of children (95.2 per cent) had watched television on the weekday evening prior to the survey.
- Over a quarter of the children in the sample had watched television for more than three and a half hours.
- Children generally reported spending significantly more time watching television than reading.
- Generally children who read most watch least television. However, nearly one-fifth of the heavy readers in the sample were also avid television viewers.
- Boys tend to watch more television than girls and report spending less time reading.
- There is a clear relationship between socio-economic background, television viewing and the amount of time spent reading.
- Nearly half of the sample (44.5 per cent) had used a computer on the evening prior to the survey.

- Nearly twice as many boys as girls had made use of a computer on the evening before the survey, and boys spent more time on the computer than girls.
- Similar percentages of children from all socio-economic groups reported using a computer.
- There was no significant relationship between the use of a computer and time spent reading in the evening prior to the survey.

Endpiece: the media and literacy

Arguments about television and reading tend to have their genesis in strongly expressed opinions that set up oppositions such as high versus popular culture, active versus passive learning, and verbal versus visual experiences. Most often television is placed on the less favoured side of the equation. As Robinson (1997) has pointed out, even the idea that television can be used to promote reading places television as the less desirable activity. This was certainly the implicit view in the first major study of television and reading in England (Himmelweit, 1955):

> The evidence suggests that television widened children's tastes in reading ... Teachers, in their capacity as parents, corroborated this finding: 'They (boys aged 8 and 9) refer to my books to find out things connected with the programmes ... Television can exert a beneficial influence by stimulating interest in a wider range of reading. This may be done indirectly, by arousing curiosity about certain fields of interest, or directly, by reviewing or dramatising books. (pp. 328–30)

Certainly many parents take the view that it is better for children to experience books than television, operating with an unquestioning assumption about the superiority of reading as somehow a superior cultural experience. Former Education Minister Michael Fallon, for example, is quoted as saying: 'I discourage Peter, who is two and a half, from watching any television. When I am home I read to him' (the *Sun* 14.5.91). It is difficult in a book devoted to understanding children's reading habits, not to fall into the position of wishing children did more reading than watching television, or wanting television to promote reading as something 'better' or 'higher'. It is our view, however, that the television or computer should not be seen in opposition to the book, but that each should be seen as one element in the range of media available to children at the end of the twentieth century. After all, it would be difficult to deny that a well-crafted television play or film is potentially at least as intellectually satisfying and culturally fulfilling as many novels. It does seem to us that the findings from various research studies, including ours, support this position: i.e. that children, on the whole, do not consider their use of different media in a hierarchical relationship with one another either in relation to the use of their spare time, or the satisfactions they gain.

It is clear, nevertheless, that the visual media have a strong influence on children's reading choices. In the early 1950s as many as one child in five had read *Jane Eyre*, a fact which Himmelweit directly relates to the dramatisation of the work on the television (Himmelweit, 1958, p. 332). There is clear evidence in our study of the influence of the media on the books children had read in the four weeks prior to the survey. Of the titles in the top 100 the following, at least, had a high media profile (usually either a cinema or television adaptation) in the five years prior to the survey date: *The BFG, The Witches, Jurassic Park, The Secret Garden, The Lion, the Witch and the Wardrobe, Madam Doubtfire, Winnie the Pooh, Watership Down, Aladdin, Jungle Book, Robin Hood, Take That, Dracula* and *Little Women*.

In the next most popular 100 titles a number of other books appear which are clearly linked to media productions: *The Wizard of Oz, The Mask, Beethoven, Honey I Shrunk/Blew Up the Kids, The Shining, Beauty and the Beast, The Pelican Brief, Frankenstein, Gremlins, Free Willy, The Crystal Maze, Batman, Star Wars, Hitchhiker's Guide to the Galaxy, Manchester United, The Little Mermaid*. Therefore approximately one in every seven books in the *Children's Reading Choices* book list of the most popular titles has some sort of media tie-in.

The children themselves, in the interviews which followed the survey, generally felt that television viewing has either no impact or an adverse impact on reading:

> Maybe, because you'll probably be more interested in the TV than reading books . . . and all these special films instead of reading books . . . and then you'll find that books get boring and you'll find TV is exciting, it's different every day. (Girl, 10)

> If you start watching *Neighbours*, you'll be watching it every day, I do. And so you might not read as much. Reading is better for you . . . more than television, because you're learning more. When you're watching television you don't really learn. (Girl, 12)

However, we have no evidence that television does change the broad shape of children's reading choices in fiction, or their reading habits. Sometimes it clearly does stimulate the reading of books. It seems to us that the generations of children who have grown up with television as just one more element in their childhood experience integrate the quite extensive use of the medium into their lives without finding it necessary to exclude other pursuits. Other surveys have made it clear that children have access to and make use of a wide range of media – and that the use of the older established ones does not invariably diminish in the face of competition with the new (e.g. Gunter and Grenberg, 1986).

One interpretation of the *Children's Reading Choices* findings is that there may be motivations, for instance towards narrative, which drive individuals to view large amounts of television, but which also push them towards other activities, including reading, to meet their particular needs. So television and reading are not necessarily in competition with one another, unless the balance between them is weighted particularly to one end of the scale. Rather, they may serve to reinforce one another – an interest in one activity may well stimulate an interest in the other. Perhaps we should be aiming to educate children to become 'media rich', having access to and making use of many media – cinema, television and computers as well as a variety of print media – to help them develop independence and balance in seeking out the variety of opportunities for learning, amusement, satisfaction and communication available through the various media.

References

Brown, J. R. *et al.*, (1974) 'Displacement effects of television and the child's functional orientation to media' in Blumler, J. and Katz, E. (eds) *The Use of Mass Communication*, Calif.: Sage

Gunter, B. and Grenberg, B. (1986) 'Media Wise', *Times Educational Supplement*, 10.10.86

Gunter, B. and McAleer, J. (1990) *Children and Television: the one eyed monster?*, London: Routledge

Himmelweit, H. *et al.* (1958) *Television and the Child*, London: Oxford University Press

Hodge, B. and Tripp, D. (1986) *Children and Television*, Oxford: Basil Blackwell

Robinson, J. P. (1969) 'Television and leisure time' *Public Opinion Quarterly*, 33, 210–22

Robinson, M. (1997) *Children Reading Print and Television*, London: Falmer Press

Chapter 8

Changes in children's reading habits over time

In this final chapter we draw further comparisons between the findings of the Whitehead team's survey in 1971 and our own replication study in the mid 1990s. We consider their recommendations and make some of our own. In the Endpiece we discuss questions of quality in children's texts, and adult responsibilities for promoting quality in relation to children's reading development.

Children and their Books, the final report of the Schools Council Children's Reading Habits project directed by Frank Whitehead from 1969–74, begins with a chapter outlining previous research into children's tastes in reading. The research team's case for their own national survey is convincingly made:

> since all the British surveys have been local in scope and limited in scale, there was a clear need in the 1970s for a national survey using a sample large enough and representative enough to justify generalizing the resultant findings to the country's children at large.
>
> (Whitehead, 1977, p. 18)

The Whitehead team argued that written questionnaires can elicit valuable information about reading habits when applied to children 10 or more years old, particularly if the questionnaires are focused primarily on obtaining factual reports of what the children have been reading in a specified length of time. In their final recommendations the team suggest that: their survey should be repeated in 1981 and then at ten-yearly intervals; a longitudinal study of the reading habits of a much smaller number of children would be desirable, and that schools should use the original questionnaire to survey their own pupils.

Children and their Books has been a very influential book since its publication in 1977. Widely read and respected, it has sparked a very large number of small scale studies and has supported teachers in understanding their pupils' reading tastes and choices. However, changes in the educational climate and funding arrangements for research during the late 70s and through the 80s did not favour the ten-yearly repetition of the national survey. The *Children's Reading Choices* survey, conducted twenty-three and a half years after the original research, therefore sets down a marker for the consideration of change in children's reading habits over a period of almost a quarter of a century.

What is probably most remarkable is the consistency of many of the surveys' findings over this period of very rapid social and cultural change. Whitehead *et al.* noted that: 'What is certainly worrying is the marked swing away from book reading as children grow older' (Whitehead, 1977, p. 272). This worry persists today amongst different sections of society. The 'swing' away from books is less marked than many commentators would suggest, but nevertheless it continues to be noteworthy, and amongst 14-year-old boys is more marked today than in the 1970s. What is not clear, is how far this mirrors adult reading habits. Are 14-year-olds replicating the gender specific reading patterns of their elders? Are adult males reading fewer books now than they were in the 1970s? Are our concerns limited to encouraging reading during the ages of statutory schooling, or do they extend to a commitment to reading as part of lifelong learning? If our commitment is to establishing reading for adult life, then it is perhaps more profitable to see 14-year-olds, most of whom are keen to establish a sense of their adult identities, as the younger end of a 14–24 cohort, rather than the older end of a 10–14 cycle.

Nevertheless, the findings related to the numbers of books read in the four weeks prior to the surveys are remarkably similar in both the *Children's Reading Choices* project and the Whitehead research. Both surveys demonstrate the link between the sex and socio-economic background of the reader, and the amount of reading being done. Both surveys provide very strong evidence of the overwhelming importance of narrative in children's reading choices. Boys' predilection for 'non-narrative' (in Whitehead's terminology) remains, although the *Children's Reading Choices* findings suggest that its significance as an element in boys' reading diet is sometimes overstated.

Hearteningly, in both surveys the most notable feature about the types of books chosen by children is their enormous diversity. Whitehead speaks of the 'extraordinary diversity of the book reading undertaken' but neither his report, nor our own experience as individual teachers and parents, had prepared us for the range and variety of texts within individuals' choices and across the age groups. Even in times of National Curriculum standardisation, and greater prescription in book lists and methods of teaching reading, Frank Whitehead's comment, made in relation to the 1971 survey, is entirely pertinent to the 1994 survey:

It seemed clear that children greatly value the opportunity given to them by book reading to exercise their own choice and to pursue highly individual interests and tastes through books. Indeed the great and continuing strength of the book in its competition with the audio-visual media (and in particular with television) is its unrivalled ability to give the individual the chance to follow his own particular bent in his own way and at his own pace at any one particular time. This opportunity for self-discovery and self-realization opened up by books seems to us an integral and central component in any conception of education which takes personal growth as its goal.

(Whitehead, 1977, p. 279)

Social and cultural change over the two decades is more evident in other parts of the research data. Patterns in periodical reading have changed significantly. Comics have given way to magazines for the older children, and a previous trend towards diminished periodical reading with age has been reversed. The periodicals themselves differ markedly from their counterparts in the 1970s. Picture strips and romantic prose fiction have been superseded by information, advice and confession fragmented into chunks which relate in a more interactive manner with elements of the visual and graphic design. The technological revolution which has taken place in the print media since the 1970s has profoundly affected reading habits because the nature, quality and quantity of magazines and newspapers has changed so radically. Children's reading habits have kept pace with the changes; school-based notions of literacy have sometimes been less adaptable.

Whitehead's team considered the children's comics 'uncouth publications', endowed with 'feebly exclamatory and emasculated' vocabulary which could 'contribute virtually nothing to the development of reading ability' (p. 285). Comics are regarded not simply as worthless but as potentially damaging:

the most deplorable aspect of this part of the 'entertainment industry' is the extent to which many children and young people have come to feel that these adult-produced and commercially motivated comics are essentially their own, a manifestation of their inner nature rather than a coarse debasement of those parts of it which can be manipulated to the greater profit of a large scale capitalist enterprise. Given such feelings (frequently evidenced in our follow up interviews) there can be no point in the school setting itself up in overt opposition to the 'culture' of the comics. The most the teacher can do is to take note of the preoccupations this culture testifies to in his pupils' make-up, and then try to find and make available as many books as he can (the more recent in publication date the better) which engage with these preoccupations in a mode which is both more sensitive and more constructive.

(Whitehead, 1977, p. 285)

This passage signifies what seems to us the most evident change over the twenty-three years between the surveys: that is, the sense of the cultural mission of the school and the teacher's role in 'improving' pupils' tastes. Whitehead's team were circumspect in making judgements about the quality of the texts the children were reading, and their respect for children would certainly prevent them from making judgements like Jenkinson's, who in a 1940 study entitled *What Do Boys and Girls Read?* focused on children's reading of 'books which would be and are read with pleasure and interest by moderately sensitive and refined adults'. Jenkinson concluded that the private reading of children aged 12–15 is 'largely chosen from inferior books, magazines and newspapers' and that children's leisure time reading was 'mainly trash by adult standards' (Jenkinson, 1940). Nevertheless, Whitehead's team took the 'admittedly somewhat controversial' step of categorising the narrative texts into 'quality' and 'non-quality' books. The criterion used to discriminate between 'quality' and 'non-quality' books is summarised thus:

Is this book one we can imagine a responsible teacher justly recommending to pupils at a certain stage of development on the ground that they are likely to take from it some imaginative experience valuable to them at their own level, over and above the mere practice of reading skills?

(Whitehead, 1977, p. 280)

Whilst the criterion does not, in itself, seem an unreasonable one to reflect upon, the idea of a consensus which would allow 'responsible' teachers to make 'just' recommendations related to an individual's imaginative development is not one which would find widespread cultural acceptance amongst teachers today. Despite his more open approach, Whitehead's definition of quality led him to arrive at similar conclusions to Jenkinson's:

at least 77 per cent of the reading of the sample consisted of narrative. It will be noticed, however, that *much of this narrative reading is of little value by adult standards* (over 45 per cent of the sample's total book reading was judged to be non-quality narrative) . . .

(Whitehead, 1987, p. 114, italics added)

Barriers between popular and élite culture are much more permeable in the 1990s than in the 1970s. The influence of multiculturalism, coupled with more varied text types as the impact of new technologies has been felt, have increased the emphasis on diversity. 'Improvement' in the late 1990s is related more closely to developing skills which allow an individual to access a range of texts and cultural practices, rather than to gaining familiarity with a canon of high cultural works. Nevertheless, these issues of quality remain important. They are discussed further in the Endpiece to this chapter.

In the 1971 survey teachers were willing to assign pupils to one of five grades for general attitude to school. Whilst, like the Whitehead team, we received tremendous amounts of help and interest from teachers, we were very aware that they would find it unacceptable to rate children in this way. Over the two decades, teachers have generally (though by no means from all quarters) been encouraged to take a more individualised view of their pupils, to differentiate their teaching and to resist simplistic categorisations. (One result of this teacher culture which surprised us was the fact that a significant number of teachers clearly objected even to pupils defining their own ethnicity, and had encouraged pupils to strike out that section of the questionnaire.) The central point here, however, is the evidence of a cultural change amongst teachers of reading: from a more consensual position in the 1970s about the cultural mission of schooling and therefore the nature of progress towards that mission, to a less consensual, more diverse view of culture and of individual progress in reading.

Children and their Books ends with a series of recommendations, most of which seem entirely appropriate today, despite the cultural, social and educational changes which have occurred in the intervening years. The fact that recommendations we would wish to make from the *Children's Reading Choices* project would be essentially similar nearly a quarter of a century after the original survey, is not, in our view, an indication of lack of progress; rather, it is an indication of the potency of reading in many children's lives, and the enduring importance of high quality teaching in supporting individual children's development.

Whitehead's team thought that 'schools and teachers need to devote more of their energies and resources to the encouragement and development of voluntary book reading over the 10–15 age range' (Whitehead, p. 285). We would endorse this recommendation, encouraging teachers to keep careful records of what children enjoy reading, and to make use of those records in discussion with the child and in making assessments of the child's progress. We are firmly convinced that teachers should accept their pupils' starting points as readers (including magazine reading amongst those starting points), working with their enthusiasms to help them build a sense of the types of reader they have been and the types of reader they might become. They should encourage conversations about things people have read, including newspaper and magazine articles.

They should offer synopses and hooks into books; they should know about teenage books and magazines. Above all, they should encourage interest, enthusiasm and a sense of purpose in reading, rather than focusing on numbers of books read. With reluctant readers particularly, each reading experience needs to be a positive one – usually leading to conversations and further recommendations for reading.

Whitehead commented that 'All schools should recognise the powerful influence they can exercise by making the right books available for leisure-time reading, and while there has undoubtedly been an improvement in provision in recent years many schools need to allocate more of their resources to the purchase of such books and to develop more expertise in their selection' (Whitehead, pp. 296–7). Clear improvements have been made in the intervening years, but nevertheless library provision is often given relatively low status in school budgets. Computer hardware and software are not alternatives to book and periodical provision in the library; they are complementary to it. Schools provide the best means of educating young people in use of the library and information services; to deny children the right to learn in school about how libraries work is to maintain inequality of access to learning resources. Many schools abandon formal teaching about library use after the pupils' first year in secondary school. Many school libraries lack sufficient modern fiction and a range of non-fiction which appeals to girls and boys. Resources need to be available to build on media tie-ins to generate enthusiasm; book ownership needs to be linked with book borrowing and school library use needs to be linked to public library use.

Children are more likely to stop reading books if their experience of reading has 'never become sufficiently enthralling or rewarding to establish a durable intrinsic motivation towards books' (Whitehead, p. 288). 'Easy reading' at a given level can be relaxing if the reader has established a reading habit. It can be useful for purposes of consolidation, or exploring a theme, or a link between characters. Ultimately, though, it is unlikely to 'enthrall' or 'reward' if the reading does not offer new challenges, new points of interest and a sense of progression. A judicious recommendation of a new author or title will move a young (or an old) reader on. An inappropriate recommendation of books that are too difficult or too mature for the child's stage of development will frustrate even the most able of readers. 'Good readers' also need to explore books written for their own age group. Whitehead points out that 'when children are making the transition from juvenile to adult books . . . they may often need to regress in terms of quality for a time concurrently with moving forward in terms of the adultness of the themes, characters or settings they read about' (p. 289). Progression is not a simple linear matter; the teacher has a key role in helping the child to explore new ideas and genres, and to build a sense of independence.

Endpiece: questions of quality and children's reading development

Commenting on the favourite books of the children surveyed in 1971, Frank Whitehead remarked upon the 'overwhelmingly nineteenth-century flavour conveyed by the list as a whole,' and for 10- and 12-year-olds particularly. Louisa May Alcott's *Little Women* was the single most popular book; it was 'only with the 14+ age group that we encounter a list where past and present mingle together on more equal terms'. The 1971 top ten books for each of the age groups are given below:

1971: 10+

Black Beauty (Anna Sewell)
Treasure Island (R. L. Stevenson)
The Secret Seven (Enid Blyton)
Little Women (Louisa M. Alcott)
Alice in Wonderland (Lewis Carroll)
The Lion, the Witch and the Wardrobe (C. S. Lewis)
Heidi (Johanna Spyri)
Robin Hood
Brer Rabbit
Tom Sawyer (Mark Twain)

1971: 12+

Little Women (Louisa M. Alcott)
Black Beauty (Anna Sewell)
Treasure Island (R. L. Stevenson)
The Lion, the Witch and the Wardrobe (C. S. Lewis)
Jane Eyre (Charlotte Brontë)
Heidi (Johanna Spyri)
Oliver Twist (Charles Dickens)
The Secret Seven (Enid Blyton)
The Silver Sword (Ian Serraillier)
Tom Sawyer (Mark Twain)

1971: 14+

Little Women (Louisa M Alcott)
Skinhead (Richard Allen)
The Day of the Triffids (John Wyndham)
Jane Eyre (Charlotte Brontë)
Animal Farm (George Orwell)

Oliver Twist (Charles Dickens)
Lord of the Flies (William Golding)
Love Story (Erich Segal)
Nineteen Eighty-Four (George Orwell)
Where Eagles Dare (Alistair Maclean)

Although a few nineteenth-century works remain popular amongst the children surveyed in the *Children's Reading Choices* research, the 1994 book lists for all ages reflect a marked emphasis on contemporary culture. The huge expansion in writing and marketing books for children and teenagers no doubt accounts, at least in part, for the change in this balance; this is not, however, the central issue we wish to pursue here. Our concern is with what these changes represent in terms of the quality of children's reading experiences, and, more particularly, the notions of high quality texts which might be most useful to teachers today. Two very perceptive commentators, Peter Benton (1995) and Elaine Millard (1997), have raised important questions about whether the decline in reading nineteenth-century 'classic' children's texts represents a drop in the quality of what children are reading (or, indeed, represents a greater honesty on the part of children completing the Benton, Millard and our own surveys!). Certainly, a strong case can be made for the importance of ensuring that children are introduced to 'classic' texts in school since they do not feature prominently in their voluntary reading choices.

Questions of quality are knotty ones for teachers. Substantial numbers of teachers in England objected vehemently to government definitions of high quality literature which became enshrined in the National Curriculum for English. Whitehead's decision, discussed earlier, to categorise the fiction children had read into 'quality' and 'non-quality' titles, also provoked controversy. 'Quality' texts were defined as 'those in which the involvement of the writer with his subject matter and his audience has been such as to generate a texture of imaginative experience which rises above the merely routine and derivative.' Non-quality books, on the other hand, were 'those whose production has been essentially a commercial operation, a matter of catering for the market'. Perhaps it is another legacy of the Thatcherite 1980s that it is so difficult to think now of authors who are not catering for the market, or mindful of the commercial side of the operation they are engaging in – or perhaps this has always been the case. In a 1987 article defending his team's categorisation and responding to some of the criticisms it had provoked, Frank Whitehead clarified the fact that he did not regard this quality/non-quality dichotomy as anything more than 'a simplifying expedient which had just enough validity to make it a useful tool for our purposes at that time' (Whitehead, 1987).

Whitehead's notions of quality and non-quality were stimulating debate fifteen years after his survey – which perhaps indicates there was 'enough validity' in his categorisation. The questions in his expanded definition are practical ones that teachers confront each time they buy books for school. But defining the quality of the valuable imaginative experience is elusive. It relies upon the reader/text interaction, but the teacher's role is to anticipate the potential quality of that interaction. And there is a danger in that, having made a judgement about a text's potential, the judgement becomes fixed as a way of categorising the text.

We need to begin with a statement of principle about quality. It seems clear to us that fundamentally the idea of quality should relate to the quality of an interaction between the text and the reader. It is possible that with any text, however banal or unpleasant or uninspiring it might seem, the interaction between the text and what the reader brings to it might result in learning which is profound and important to the individual concerned. So, for example, a reader coming to the small print of an insurance policy or a child completing an independent reading of a *Famous Five* novel might have high quality reading experiences at certain key moments. Fundamentally, then, we want to say that reading is a dialogic activity, and that the notion of quality should be applied to the reading experience itself.

However, we also think that such a notion of quality is limited in its utility for those with responsibility for supporting children's reading development. Teachers, librarians and parents cannot sidestep the question of quality insofar as it relates to particular texts, for a set of rather obvious reasons. First, these adults hold the purse-strings; they purchase the children's books which are found on shelves at home or in school or in the library. At the point of purchase, the quality of individual children's reading experiences with the text is an act of imagination – informed probably by experience, but nonetheless a projection into the future. The adult brings to the choice a set of judgements about the applicability of the story content to the children's situation, about the level of textual difficulty and the length of the book, about the price, etc. All of which might be adduced as elements relating to the *suitability* of a book. But we want to argue that there is another element in play in this decision making, and that relates to a judgement being made about the quality of the text under consideration – a quality which resides in the text itself.

The notion of quality residing in a text is well established, of course, and it is only relatively recent literary critical approaches which have rendered it problematic. It is not, however, a concept that has in itself been well defined. It has always relied rather heavily upon a circular notion that the quality of fiction is determined by readers of discernment and good taste, and that good quality fiction is what these readers like to read. By extension, good quality children's fiction is generally what adult 'discerning' readers choose for their offspring.

Since our starting position is that high quality reading experiences can arise from an interaction between a reader and virtually any text, our view is that it is unhelpful to adopt a negative, deficit model of children's reading choices. It is better to consider what children do get from the reading they enjoy doing, and then to think of ways of supplementing and extending those benefits by introducing new material. The notion of children's literature as a substandard branch of adult literature encourages a reading scheme approach to books – a sense that you move through them as quickly as possible to arrive at the goal. And such an approach does not foster broadly developmental approaches to the reading process.

From these starting points, our focus is on two strands which seem to us neglected in the debates about quality in literature. We wish to consider the quality of texts in relation to two central features: the narrative complexity and the 'literariness' of the language. Our suspicion is that these two strands – along with judgements about suitability of subject matter and layout – could focus some of the rather vague judgements about quality which many of us operate with. They could help sharpen judgements made about what a text potentially has to offer, and offer a framework for developing the range and sophistication of children's reading.

We can only sketch in our supporting arguments here, but what we are aiming for is a set of criteria for thinking about quality which helps define what a text might offer a child and, therefore, enables an adult to consider ways of helping the child create a varied and challenging reading diet. We aim to sketch out our arguments by relating them to two novels for children: *The BFG* by Roald Dahl which is the most popular book in the 1994 survey, and *Little Women* by Louisa M. Alcott, which was most popular in the 1971 Whitehead survey.

Our argument for the importance of considering narrative complexity rests on Barbara Hardy's thesis that narrative is a primary act of mind, and that therefore increasingly complex narrative structures offer frames for more complex ways of thinking (Hardy, 1987). Following Margaret Donaldson, we believe that a prime function of education is to develop 'disembedded' more abstract ways of thinking, and that appreciation of patterned discourse and varieties of narrative structures can help children develop their capacities for that kind of abstract thought (Donaldson, 1987). What can we say about *The BFG* and *Little Women* in this respect? We have used Genette's work on narratology to offer a language and analytical frame for thinking about the text structures (Genette, 1980).

Little Women has a simple chronological pattern, tightly controlled, with the story beginning one Christmas and ending the next. The story is centred in one household – only two other households are shown in the book, and these only insofar as they have a bearing on the March family household. There are very few subordinate story-lines – a war is going on, but is not elaborated upon; the poor Hummel family occur twice, but their story of hardship works only in relation to March family charity. The most fully developed subplot is the reported tale of Laurie's parents and the breakdown of their relationship with Laurie's grandfather. The implications of this provide the subtext to the grandfather's attitude to music, and hence Beth, and his authoritarian behaviour towards his grandson which furthers the motif of maintaining a secure family group.

The pace, or in Genette's terms, the 'duration' of the story is fairly steady: that is, there is a balance between the amount written and the length of time covered in the story. There is very little ellipsis in the story telling, there are few descriptive pauses but a good deal of dialogue. The point of view of the narrative is that of an omniscient narrator external to the characters in the story, but with a female voice, highly approving of the family – a kind of meta-Mrs March figure, who shares her philosophy and whose motherliness extends to the readers as well as the March family. There is therefore a distance between the narration and the story, but no disjunction (anachronies).

> I don't think I have any words in which to tell the meeting of the mother and daughters; such hours are beautiful to live, but very hard to describe, so I will leave it to the imagination of my readers . . .
>
> (Alcott, originally 1868, p. 258)

or

> As young readers like to know 'how people look', we will take this moment to give them a little sketch of the four sisters . . .
>
> (p. 14)

The BFG is also a simple chronological narrative but it offers some degree of narrative complexity in the final chapter 'The Author', when there is the suggestion that it is the giant who has written the story using the pen-name Roald Dahl. This device is used simply, but it offers an example of what Genette calls external analepsis – that is the creation of a secondary, subordinate narrative (in this case about learning to write and succeeding in writing a book) which in temporal terms stands outside of the main narrative. There is a shift in that the narrator, seemingly standing outside of the story throughout, is, at the end, placed within it as the act of narration is brought to the fore. There are variations in the rhythm of the narrative: there is some implicit ellipsis between chapters, some summary as the giant and Sophie make their journey, and a skilful use of simple anticipation (prolepsis):

Suddenly she froze. *There was something coming up the street on the opposite side.*
It was something black . . .
Something tall and black . . .
Something very tall and very black and very thin.

(Dahl, 1982, p. 11)

There is a lot more to say about the narrative complexities of both books, but our argument at this point is that this kind of analysis offers a way into thinking about the quality of a text which encourages a detailed, reflective approach rather than a broad brush sweep which results in the 'good quality/dubious quality' distinction. Or indeed, the 'valuable/ worthless' distinction. There are interesting points about the narration of both texts. Children of varying ages and ability levels can think and talk about the structures with varying degrees of sophistication – the quality of both books provides the basis for such work.

The other strand of our argument, about literary language, allows us to touch on issues of canonical and non-canonical literature. Clearly it is important for children to encounter a wide range of different forms of written language. In relation to fiction reading, however, 'literary' language is particularly privileged, and 'literature' is clearly a category of writing which confers cultural capital. Children have the right to learn something about the literary heritage and canonical texts of their own culture, and indeed other cultures. Access to these texts, but also to a great many others, is improved by a reader's familiarity and ease with the conventions of literary language. We are therefore proposing that there is value in considering how literary language plays its part in the notion of quality.

What, in practice, does it mean to consider the literariness of language? Ron Carter and Walter Nash's book *Seeing Through Language* (1990) is helpful here. Carter and Nash take the Russian Formalists' suggestion that literary language is 'deviant' language insofar as it departs or deviates from expected configurations and normal patterns with the effect of defamiliarising the reader. Literary language is often self referential; 'phonoaesthetic patterning' (for example, assonance, repetition, alliteration) is likely to feature. A 'more literary' text is likely to have greater semantic density – that is, superimposed codes and levels within the text which interact with one another. This interactive patterning might be at the level of lexis, syntax, phonology or discourse. Polysemy – the suggestion that a text should be read in more than one way – is a feature of literary texts; denotations are always potentially available for transformation into connotations. Literary texts often have a feeling of speech about them, with a sense of the text as interaction. Features of the text might also be plurisignifying, in their capacity to be memorable and promote intertextual relations and provide verbal pleasure, so that they are frequently cited and become embedded in new discourses.

Thinking about this in relation to the quality of *Little Women*, we can observe that 'deviant' literary language is employed, sometimes simply and sometimes more metaphorically (chapter 6):

> The big house did prove a Palace Beautiful, though it took some time for all to get in, and Beth found it very hard to pass the lions.

The whole text works in conjunction with a reading of *The Pilgrim's Progress*. Explicit mentions of *The Pilgrim's Progress* are made throughout, in the text and in chapter titles; copies of the book are given as gifts within the plot, the girls play a game of being pilgrims, and Bunyan's imagery is drawn upon in the writing, as in the quotation cited above. The text is carefully patterned to show each of the four sisters shouldering the burden of her particular personality trait. The nature of her journey is made explicit at the start and her progress is commented upon by the mother throughout and by the father on his return at the end of the novel.

There is a good deal in *Little Women* about language – Amy's malapropisms throughout, for example – and a lot about story telling. Mrs March at one point creates highly moralistic tales from the girls' accounts of their days' work. This process could almost be seen as offering a paradigm of the novel as a whole. Jo's comment to her mother might be echoed to the author by the reader (p. 66):

> It is very cunning of you to . . . give us a sermon instead of a romance.

The characters tell, write and read stories, and there is an open interactive quality throughout as the reader is invited to listen and respond – most notably at the end, where Louisa Alcott (with a clear eye on her sales figures?) invites the audience to demand a sequel (p. 303):

> So grouped, the curtain falls upon Meg, Jo, Beth and Amy.
> Whether it ever rises again, depends upon the reception
> given to the first act of the domestic drama called
> LITTLE WOMEN.

The BFG is also a polysemic text, but it works as a fairy tale about big and small lonely people. The novel raises expectations of readings against other fairy tales, and against stories in which evil giants are vanquished and Queens sort things out. There is an interactive quality to the writing, made explicit through addresses to the reader such as (p. 17):

If you can think of anything more terrifying than that happening to you in the middle of the night, then let's hear about it.

Deviant language is a central feature of *The BFG*: the text is rich in verbal play throughout. However, the deviant language is almost entirely located within the speech characteristics of the big friendly giant. There is a great sense of pleasure and fun in the giant's use of language, but ultimately the structure of the text as a whole validates conformity and learning the 'correct' use of language (the giant becomes the author of the successful book we have just read). The following passage illustrates a tension that runs throughout: the giant's language is creative, comprehensible and imaginative, the child is bound by good manners and her own intelligence to accept the giant's language, but in the end his language won't do (pp. 48–50):

The BFG looked at Sophie and smiled, showing about twenty of his square white teeth. 'Yesterday,' he said, 'we was not believing in giants, was we? Today we is not believing in snozzcumbers. Just because we happen not to have actually seen something with our own two little winkles, we think it is not existing. What about for instance the great squizzly scotch-hopper?'

'I beg your pardon?' Sophie said.

'And the humplecrimp?'

'What's that?' Sophie said.

'And the wraprascal?'

'The what?' Sophie said.

'And the crumpscoddle?'

'Are they animals?' Sophie asked.

'They is *common* animals,' said the BFG contemptuously. 'I is not a very know-all giant myself, but it seems to me that you is an absolutely know-nothing human bean. Your brain is full of rotten-wool.'

'You mean cotton-wool,' Sophie said.

'What I mean and what I say is two different things,' the BFG announced rather grandly. 'I will now show you a snozzcumber.'

The BFG flung open a massive cupboard and took out the weirdest looking thing Sophie had ever seen. It was about half as long again as an ordinary man but was much thicker. It was as thick around its girth as a perambulator. It was black with white stripes along its length. And it was covered all over with coarse knobbles.

'Here is the repulsant snozzcumber!' cried the BFG, waving it about. 'I squoggle it! I mispise it! I dispunge it! But because I is refusing to gobble up human beans like the other giants, I must spend my life guzzling up icky-poo snozzcumbers instead. If I don't I will be nothing but skin and groans.'

'You mean skin and *bones*,' Sophie said.

'I *know* it is bones,' the BFG said. 'But please understand that I cannot be helping it if I sometimes is saying things a little squiggly. I is trying my very best all the time.' The Big Friendly Giant looked suddenly so forlorn that Sophie got quite upset.

'I'm sorry,' she said. 'I didn't mean to be rude.'

'There never was any schools to teach me talking in Giant Country,' the BFG said sadly.

Textual patterning related to the theme of eating habits allows for the verbal invention – 'snozzcumbers' and 'whizzpoppers', etc. – which many children find very funny. These items certainly provide verbal pleasure, and many teachers and parents can testify to the plurisignifying qualities of words like 'whizzpopper', which become embedded in alternative discourses.

To summarise some of these points about literary language and quality, we could compare the two texts we are considering and suggest that both have something to offer in helping readers become familiar with literary conventions. In both texts there are elements of verbal play and discussion about the uses of language and the act of storytelling which employ 'deviant' unfamiliar language and promote intertextual connections. *The BFG* is a text which is simpler in several respects. First, in that the intertextual connections are to a simpler and generic story form rather than a specific 'classic' text – *The Pilgrim's Progress*. Second, in that the more deviant, more 'literary' language is located within a character's speech patterns rather than within the language of the text as a whole. Both *The BFG* and *Little Women* are texts with markedly 'literary' qualities; *Little Women*, against the criteria we are using, is more sophisticated in its use of literary language.

Which is not, of course, to seek generally to promote the reading of one text over the other. In some respects, since re-reading is popular amongst children, we want to suggest helping them focus on different elements during different readings. This would be a useful part of overseeing reading development since the texts lend themselves differently to more or less sophisticated readings. It is too simplistic to consider content and genre as the predominating features of judgements about quality. The author's commercialism seems irrelevant to the judgement. And trying to pin down the notion of potential imaginative experience is too vague.

Carter and Nash use the idea of a 'cline' of literariness, a gradation of stylistic and discursive qualities which mark some texts as more 'literary' than others. Similarly, one might imagine a cline of narrative complexity, with some texts being acknowledged as structurally more complex and sophisticated than others. And both of those clines would give us ways of talking about the qualities of the texts we were offering to children which avoid the adult tendency to decry the value of texts that children choose to read, and which simultaneously build in a broad notion of reading development rather than a leap-frogging from one quality assured text to another.

References

Alcott, L. M. (1995) *Little Women*, London: Penguin

Benton, P. (1995) 'Recipe Fictions: Literary Fast Food? Reading Interests in Yr 8', *Oxford Review of Education*, vol. 21, 108–11.

Bunyan, J. (1971 edition) *The Pilgrim's Progress*, London: Penguin

Carter, R. and Nash, W. (1990) *Seeing Through Language*, Oxford: Blackwell

Dahl, R. (1982) *The BFG*, London: Penguin

Donaldson, M. (1987) *Children's Minds*, London: Fontana

Genette, G. (1980) *Narrative Discourse: an Essay in Method*, New York: Cornell University Press

Hardy, B. (1987) 'Narrative as a Primary Act of Mind' in *The Collected Essays of Barbara Hardy*, Brighton: Harvester Press

Jenkinson, A. J. (1940) *What Do Boys and Girls Read?*, London: Methuen

Millard, E. (1997) *Differently Literate*, London: Falmer Press

Whitehead, F. (1987) '"Quality" Revisited' in *English in Education*, vol. 23, 3

Whitehead, F. *et al.* (1977) *Children and Their Books*, London: Macmillan

Appendix I

The questionnaire

PUPIL'S QUESTIONNAIRE

What this booklet is for

Many people who take part in your education would like to know what kinds of books you are interested in reading and what other things you like doing.

This questionnaire is to help schools, publishers, libraries and book-sellers provide the most suitable and enjoyable books for you.

Why you have been chosen to fill in the booklet

Obviously we can't ask everybody who is at school to fill in a booklet; that would take too long and be very expensive. So we got a computer to take a list of all schools and picked out one school of every sort in each part of the country. Then we took a list of all the pupils of a certain age in each of these schools and chose a number of them in a way that was rather like picking numbers out of a hat. You are one of the pupils who were chosen in this way and it is very important to us that you should fill in the answers to the questions as carefully as you can.

We need you to tell us what really goes on, so please don't just write what you think adults want to hear.

Thank you for your help.

How to fill in the booklet

For some of the questions we will give you a set of answers and you will have to choose one that is right for you by putting a tick in the box next to it, like this: ☑ You will only have to put *one* tick in *one* of the boxes.

For other questions, you have to write out the answer. You won't need to write very much and there will be a box to write in.

Your answers will be completely private. Also do remember that this isn't an examination or a test, so don't worry about spelling.

Your teacher will help you if you have any difficulties.

1   Do you regularly read any magazines, comics or newspapers?

(a) Put a tick ☑ in the box by the answer you choose.

☐ Yes
If you answer 'Yes' write a
list of all the magazines,
comics or newspapers you
read. Write only one on
each line. If you only read
one or two, put those down.

☐ No
If you answer 'No'
go on to question 2.

(b) Read down your list and put a tick ☑ after the one you most
look forward to reading. Now go on to question 2.

2   Have you read a book (or books) in the last four weeks?
Don't count books which a teacher said you must read as part of a
lesson or for homework.

☐ Yes
If you answer 'Yes'
carry on with the
next question.

☐ No
If you answer 'No'
go on to question
9.

3   Which books have you read in the last four weeks?
Write down any books you got outside school and any you chose
yourself from school. Don't put down books which a teacher said
you must read as part of a lesson or for homework.

   Now, write down all the books that you have read in the last four
weeks. Put the author's name as well, if you can. It doesn't matter if
you can't remember all of the books you have read or if you have
only read one or two books.

   (We've written down two books to show you how to do it.)

TITLE	AUTHOR
Gold That Glitters	E. Holt
A Twenty Year Secret	W. West

4   Have you read any of the books you've put down more than once?
If you have go back and underline it, like this:

Gold That Glitters

5   Did you decide not to finish any of the books?

If you stopped reading a book before the end put a cross after the title, like this:

A Twenty Year Secret X

Now, for every book you've written down in question 3 choose *one* of the answers to question 6 and *one* of the answers to question 7.

  Put a tick on the same line as the book under the answer you choose. (We've put ticks next to our books to show you how to do it.)

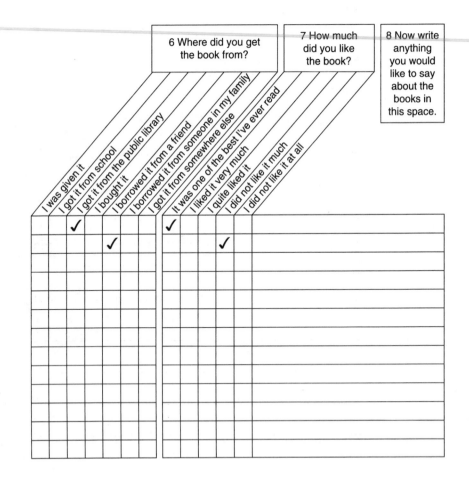

9   Do you own any books yourself?

☐ Yes   ☐ No
   If you answer 'Yes' put a   If you answer 'No'
   tick in the box which is   go on to question 10.
   nearest to the number of
   books you own.

☐ I own up to 10 books

☐ I own between 11 and 25 books

☐ I own between 26 and 50 books

☐ I own between 51 and 100 books

☐ I own more than 100 books

10   About how many books are there in your home?

☐ hardly any   ☐ a few   ☐ quite a lot   ☐ lots

11(a) Do you have a favourite writer, or a favourite series of books?

☐ Yes   ☐ No
   If you answer 'Yes'   If you answer 'No' go
   write the name.   on to question 12.

```



```

(b)   What first gave you the idea to read this author or series of
       books?

```



```

12 About how much reading do you think you do?

Put a tick in the box by the answer you choose.

☐ A large amount

☐ Quite a lot

☐ About average

☐ Not very much

☐ Only a little

13 Do you think you are good at reading?

Put a tick in the box by the answer you choose.

☐ very good

☐ good

☐ average

☐ not very good

☐ poor

14 Do you borrow books from the public library?

Put a tick in the box by the answer you choose.

☐ Yes   ☐ No
   If you answer 'Yes' tick   If you answer 'No' go on
   the answer which is most   to question 15.
   nearly true for you.

☐ I go to borrow books about once a week

☐ I go to borrow books about once every two weeks

☐ I go to borrow books about once a month

☐ I go to borrow books only sometimes

15 Did you watch television last night?

(It doesn't matter whether it was at home or somewhere else.)

☐ Yes
If you answer 'Yes' for
how long did you watch?

☐ No
If you answer 'No' go on
to question 16.

☐ Less than ½ hour

☐ Between ½ hour and 1½ hours

☐ Between 1½ hours and 2½ hours

☐ Between 2½ hours and 3½ hours

☐ More than 3½ hours

16 Did you do any reading last night?

(It doesn't matter what it was or whether it was at home or somewhere else.)

☐ Yes
If you answer 'Yes' for
how long did you read?

☐ No
If you answer 'No' go on
to question 17.

☐ Less than ½ hour

☐ Between ½ hour and 1½hours

☐ Between 1½ hours and 2½ hours

☐ Between 2½ hours and 3½ hours

☐ More than 3½ hours

17 Did you use a computer, or play any computer games last night?

(It doesn't matter whether it was at home or somewhere else.)

☐ Yes
If you answer 'Yes' for how
long?

☐ No
If you answer 'No' go on
to Question 18.

☐ Less than ½ hour

☐ Between ½ hour and 1½ hours

☐ Between 1½ hours and 2½ hours

☐ Between 2½ hours and 3½ hours

☐ More than 3½ hours

18(a) Have you bought any books, comics, magazines or newspapers this year (1994)?

☐ Yes
If you answer 'Yes' which shop did you buy them from? Please write down the names of any shops you have used.

☐ No
If you answer 'No' go on to question 19.

Name of shop	Book	Comic	Magazine	Newspaper

(b) Now go back and put a tick in the boxes which will tell us whether you bought a book, or a comic, or a magazine, or a newspaper, or all four.

19

Now make a list of the adults you live with. (under here)	Is the person male or female? Write M or F. (under here)	If any of these adults go out to work write down what their job is. (under here)	Do any of these adults read a lot at home? If yes put a tick for them. (under here)

20

Now make a list of any children you live with. (under here)	Is the person male or female? Write M or F. (under here)	Write down their ages. (under here)	Do any of these children read a lot? If yes put a tick for them. (under here)

21(a) Do you speak a language other than English at home?

☐ Yes.
If you answer 'Yes'
carry on with the next
question

☐ No.
If you answer 'No', go
on to question 22.

(b) Can you write in this language? ☐ Yes ☐ No

(c) Can you read in this language? ☐ Yes ☐ No

(d) Is it easy to find things you enjoy
reading in this language? ☐ Yes ☐ No

22 How would you describe yourself?
(For example, Chinese, White, Asian, Black-British, etc.)

┌─────────────────────────────────────┐
│   │
└─────────────────────────────────────┘

23 Are you a boy or a girl?

☐ boy

☐ girl

24 How old are you?
Put your age, in years, in the box.
☐

25 Please complete this sentence with one or two words

I think that reading is _

Thank you very much for your help.

Pupil's questionnaire: administration procedures

1 This questionnaire should be completed on either a Tuesday, Wednesday, Thursday or Friday by those children for whom it is intended (please see covering letter for details), and returned by **4 July**.

2 We anticipate that it will take pupils between   and   minutes to complete the questionnaire. We would be grateful if you could allow longer for pupils who may need it.

3 To encourage the pupils to be as frank as possible, we have told them that their answers will be completely private. We would be grateful if the teacher administering the questionnaire could lend strength to this assurance by removing the questionnaires in front of the pupils and replacing them when they have been completed.

4 In general we ask the teacher who administers the questionnaire to show as little interest as possible in the content of pupils answers, and to confine his or her aid to those difficulties which the pupils cannot resolve themselves. Some pupils may need special help with reading and responding to the questionnaire. We are happy for staff to assist pupils in whatever way is appropriate to their individual needs. It is important for the accuracy of the data that pupils do not discuss their responses with their friends.

5 Before pupils start answering, we would be grateful if the **instructions on the first page** of the questionnaire could be read aloud to all pupils. You may decide that it is appropriate to read aloud all instructions.

6 We ask that you call attention to the phrase 'in the last four weeks' **in questions 2 and 3**. Some pupils may have difficulty in conceptualizing this period of time, and it would be useful to mention any local circumstance which would help fix it in their minds.

7 We anticipate that **questions 3–8** may need some explaining in terms of their arrangement on the page.

8 **Questions 10, 11 and 12** relate to **pupils' perceptions** of the books available to them, their reading behaviours and abilities. The categories do not relate to specific numbers, amounts or assessment objectives.

9 We have liaised with the Council for Racial Equality about **questions 21 and 22** on second languages and ethnicity. They have approved the design and phrasing of these two questions. For **question 22** we would like to emphasise that we require the information in terms of how the pupils would describe themselves. However, we anticipate that some pupils may seek guidance here.

Finally, if the pupils experienced any difficulties in completing the questionnaire, could you briefly outline the nature of these difficulties overleaf?

Thank you very much for your help.

Project procedures

Questionnaire construction

The questionnaire was constructed to mirror Whitehead's investigation insofar as this was possible. This replication would allow us to gather data which would enable analysis of change over time. Our overriding concern in the design was to ensure that the questions asked investigated the choices that children make in their reading. However, we decided to jettison one major area of Whitehead's survey: the element which was concerned directly with the influence of the school. Much of the school-based information which was important in the educational context of the 1970s was no longer applicable to the context of the 1990s. We added extra questions about computer use, purchasing patterns and family reading habits.

The pilot survey

The purpose of the pilot was to ensure that there would be no problems with the procedures for distribution, administration and completion of the questionnaire during the main survey. It was not the purpose of the pilot to establish preliminary findings. The sample was too small and may not have been representative.

Eight schools were selected using the principles which underpinned the sampling in the main survey. Seven agreed to participate in the research. Two-hundred and fifty questionnaires were returned within the time requested. None of the schools reported any problems with the administration of the questionnaire. Inspection of the responses suggested that although the children had no serious problems in completing the questionnaire, revisions were necessary to the layout and design of some of the questions to facilitate the retrieval of information. No further revision of the questionnaire was therefore considered necessary.

Schools appreciated the preliminary 'priming' letters which were followed by telephone conversations to explain the project and confirm arrangements. Procedures for packaging, postage and return were problematic. These procedures were modified and a contract with Royal Mail was drawn up.

Sample construction

The final sampling strategy resulted from a combination of considerations. Reflecting the overall study aims, the sample nature needed to replicate, as far as possible, that of the original survey. We also needed to take full account of the current school climate, and the pressures on teachers' time and energies. In the event, however, the level of support from teachers was extremely generous, and there was considerable enthusiasm for the study, so that the final samples were rather larger than expected.

Whitehead's original study employed a two-stage probabilistic approach, sampling from all schools in England and Wales except those from authorities adopting a middle-school policy, and also excluding single-sex primary schools and independent schools. The first stage involved the selection of these schools using a procedure which ensured proportionate representation that correctly reflected the numbers of schools of different sizes. The second stage determined the manner in which the pupils were selected. First, target ages of 10, 12 and 14 were set. Then appropriate numbers of pupils from the selected schools were identified. The general aim of the strategy was to represent all school sizes and types, all LEAs, and the selected pupil age ranges. It was inferred from that strategy that implicit variables such as socio-economic indicators, school policies, pupil ability and sex would be similarly represented.

We accepted the need to achieve this degree of representativeness but we were aware of major limitations that needed to be accommodated. First, at the national level, it would not have been possible to obtain the extensive assistance originally accorded by the Department for Education and Science in constructing the probabilistic sample. Expensive provision of this kind is not often provided at no cost (as it was then) and the actual costs would have been prohibitive. We needed a less costly scheme that could achieve the same end. Within schools there have also been major changes in what researchers can reasonably expect of teachers and pupils. In particular the organisational demands needed to be kept to a minimum. So we did not require teachers or schools to do more that identify target classes. Second, we avoided disruption of schools and teaching by working with whole classes.

As far as the outcomes are concerned, we have no reason to doubt the effectiveness of this strategy. So long as the population is not too disparate (and modern school populations are more homogeneous than in 1971) cluster sampling is at least as reliable as systematic or random sampling.

By virtually eliminating external involvement in sample selection we avoided the possibility (albeit small) of teacher bias. Checks on indicators such as sex and ethnicity are available within the reporting of the results.

The strategy adopted for school selection consisted of sampling from selected local authorities, maintaining representativeness by school size. The LEAs were chosen to span the main socio-economic regions typically recognised in educational and social research. The dominant descriptors here are rural, metropolitan and London, with qualifiers such as suburban and relative affluence allowing a more refined characterisation. The fifteen LEAs ultimately selected are shown in Table A-1 summarising the secondary sample. Selecting authorities with a set initial letter (here 'H') is a neat but simple randomisation device. Including the North-East allowed a range of rural, industrial and urban localities to feature. Avon was selected for similar reasons, but in the expectation that it would show different characteristics. The overall population covered by these regions is about 8.3 million, so it does comprise almost one-fifth of England. The sample design is illustrated on the table.

The next step was to obtain data on the relative incidences of different-sized schools. Compiling these data from the published listings proved extremely time consuming, and somewhat unreliable with so much missing information. The Department for Education was able to supply us with breakdowns by authority and size, and we were extremely grateful to them for this assistance. The results are shown in the table. From that point on it became a matter of extrapolating from likely response rates, school class sizes and desired final sample size. We estimated that about 75 per cent of schools would participate, which led us to start from a sample of 100 secondary schools. The distributions across the LEAs are as shown, the proportions relating to actual population proportions. The selection of schools by size was simplified by the fact that the three size-bands we operated (splitting at 700 and 900) occurred almost equally.

Our selection of pupils was simplified considerably by using intact classes. The relevant ages determined which school year was to be involved. In order to achieve acceptable spread we requested two classes per school. The classes themselves were tutor groups rather than subject groups. This ensured even better representation since any possible ability or sex bias was avoided. The only drawback in this approach was that numbers of pupils involved were higher than originally planned.

The procedures used for the primary schools were analogous to the secondary school procedures. The only operational differences were the school-size cut-off points, and the inclusion of only one class per school (that containing the 10-year-old pupils).

The sample was designed to be usable at several levels. The maintenance of representativeness across characteristics such as region and

A-1 Children's Reading Choices project – sample design: secondary

	Pop. (m.)	School size range	Data on school sizes across England						Totals	Sample needed
			0–499	500–699	700–899	900–1,099	1,100–1,299	1,300–		
Initial 'H'	0.99	Hertfordshire	12	14	28	14	4	0	72	11
	0.86	Humberside	3	12	15	11	10	8	59	9
		3-band totals		41	43	47			131	20
North-East	0.59	Durham	2	10	13	6	4	0	35	5
	0.57	Cleveland	8	10	11	4	4	2	39	5
	0.16	South Tyneside	0	4	3	1	1	0	9	2
	0.75	North Yorkshire	18	16	13	5	5	3	60	8
		3-band totals		68	40	35			143	20
London 'H' about 10% pop.	0.19	Hackney	0	2	5	2	0	0	9	3
	0.23	Havering	2	5	6	3	3	0	19	7
	0.2	Hounslow	0	1	6	4	1	2	14	5
		3-band totals		10	17	15			42	15
Home Counties	1	Surrey	8	18	8	6	5	3	48	7.5
	0.75	Berkshire	11	11	9	8	6	3	48	7.5
		3-band totals		48	17	31			96	15
Avon	0.95	Avon	3	11	13	20	8	4	59	10
		3-band totals		14	13	32			59	10
Metropolitan	0.44	Manchester City	0	0	3	10	2	2	17	6
	0.31	Wakefield	3	5	6	2	2	1	19	7
	0.31	Wigan	0	7	3	6	3	2	21	7
		3-band totals		15	12	30			57	20
		Overall totals	72	134	159	111	62	32	571	100
		3-band overall		206	159	206			571	100

Notes 1 Approximate national population figures give London 8m., metropolitan boroughs 10m., leaving the rest at about 30m. This means that the sample is split roughly as follows: London 15 per cent, metropolitan boroughs 20 per cent and the rest 65 per cent.

2 The authorities selected above allow us to cover the three main areas of London, Metropolitan and the rest and give the flexibility of comparing London with Metropolitan and different areas of the rest (e.g. South vs. North-East).

3 The samples-needed column shows a rough indication of the numbers from each authority for contact purposes (e.g. 100 to give 75).

4 The three size bands are very nearly one third splits. This makes it easier to ensure that the three sizes are represented.

size means that each unit can be analysed separately, as well as within the complete nationally representative sample. With very large samples such as this one, statistical significance can be so readily achieved that emphasis becomes more difficult to decide. Analysing smaller sub-samples allows a more refined analysis specification (i.e. more variables together) whilst still maintaining statistical reliability.

The main survey procedures

We designed a comprehensive database for all schools in the sample. Each school was identifiable by a number which included codes for each phase (primary or secondary), each sector (state or independent), size of school, geographical region, urban or rural location and single or mixed sex intake.

During the week commencing 5 September 1994, schools identified in the sample received an introductory letter requesting their assistance. In the weeks commencing 12 and 19 September, a small team of researchers followed up those letters with a telephone call to each school to establish whether it was willing to participate in the project. In the first instance contact was made with the headteacher. In the case of secondary schools, further telephone conversations took place with the head of the English department. The calls were used to establish information on pupil groupings, urban or rural locations and the number of questionnaires to be provided. The procedures for administering the questionnaires were discussed. Schools' information was recorded on the database and all calls were logged.

A package was then despatched to the contact person in each school, containing a set of instructions and a follow-up letter. Each package contained a pre-paid label for return by 21 October 1994. A return slip was also included for schools to record the number of questionnaires returned in each age category.

The returned packages were recorded and matched with the database so that a check could be kept on total returns. Reminder telephone calls were made to those schools who failed to make a return by the due date.

After the initial response the research team identified from the returns that responses from 12-year-olds were under-represented. We therefore targeted the relevant schools to ensure equality of response across the age categories.

Over 9,000 questionnaires were distributed. The return rate was 89 per cent giving a total return of 7,976 (10-year-olds = 2,975, 12-year-olds = 2,455, 14-year-olds = 2,546).

The interview phase of the project

The interview phase of the project took place between 6 June and 14 July 1995. We aimed to interview 1 per cent of the total sample: in the event 87 children were interviewed (just over 1 per cent of the sample). The distribution of the ages of the pupils was as shown in Table A-2.

We approached schools that had participated in the main survey, selecting our sample from different regions of England according to the divisions into metropolitan, London and other areas that we had operated with in the construction of the original stratified random sample. The schedule of visits is given in Table A-3.

We decided that one interviewer should conduct all of the pupil interviews to maintain reliability, and to allow development of ideas and investigations over the range of interviews. The interviewer we chose is an experienced teacher, skilled at working in one-to-one relationships with children. She had worked on the *Children's Reading Choices* project from its inception: contacting schools, dispatching, following up and receiving questionnaires, coding 2,000 of them and contributing to discussions about the interview schedule.

Table A-2

Age (years)	No. of girls	No. of boys	Total
10+	15	15	30
12+	14	14	28
14+	15	14	29
Total	44	43	87

Table A-3

Date	Area	No. of primary school pupils	No. of secondary school pupils
8 June	Home Counties	5	
9 June	Home Counties		9
13 June	Humberside	5	
14 June	Humberside		10
19 June	London	4	
20 June	London		8
26 June	Avon	6	
27 June	Avon		10
6 July	Manchester		10
7 July	Manchester	5	
13 July	Cleveland	5	
14 July	Cleveland		10
Total		30	57

In early May the interview schedule was piloted with six children to check, particularly, the timing and the suitability of the language levels, and the recording procedures. The pilot tape-recordings formed the basis of detailed discussions between the interviewer and the project team, after which procedures and exact wordings were agreed.

We chose a semi-structured interview format to allow a clear structure with enough flexibility to enable the interviewer to respond to the children's points and to follow up interesting and unforeseen responses. Interviews took place in school in a quiet room set aside by the school for the purpose. Pupils were excused from lessons to be interviewed. The actual pupils chosen were randomly selected on the basis of having a birthday on or very soon after 1 January; depending upon the number of pupils we wanted to interview from the school, we chose them in birthday order. We intended by this means to keep the age differentials consistent. Pupils were asked whether they wished to be interviewed. Once the purposes of the exercise were made clear, none refused.

All interviews were tape-recorded, with the children's permission, and the interviewer also took notes according to the schedule we had devised. The interview schedule is appended. After the interview period, the interviewer collated and wrote up the data in a descriptive form from her notes, including illustrative transcription material. The analysis of the data was carried out by the main project team.

The statistical analysis

The questionnaire responses were processed to facilitate analysis by two separate strategies. First, the listings of items such as book titles and purchase outlets were retained as text information. They were organised and analysed using a word processing program.

The second strategy involved the use of quantitative analysis wherever the questionnaire items were suitable. In many instances the questions had been offered with categorised response options and these responses were translated directly into numeric codes. Similarly, where responses were themselves numbers, either these numbers or recoded versions were used in the analyses. Finally, for some questions, a new numeric code was generated in the form of a count or some similar coding procedure. The numeric data were coded and entered for computer analysis by the statistical package SPSS-X Version 3 (SPSS Inc, 1988).

Preliminary analysis consisted of generating descriptive statistics (essentially frequency distributions) for all the coded items (i.e. variables). In the second stage the research questions were addressed in a series of two-way cross-tabulations. With such a large number of variables in the questionnaire, some selection was necessary for manageability. Various pupil indicators (especially sex, age, socio-economic and ethnic background) presented a major focus for the selection of tables whereby these variables were compared with other questions comprising the essence of the survey. Findings from the previous survey, and indications from statistical significance tests, were also used as a basis for the tabular selection. It is important to emphasise that in this particular survey statistical significance could by itself be used as an indicator of educational significance. The very large sample necessarily leads to an excessively high number of significant tables (when tested using chi-square) within the normal conventions of probability levels of 0.05 and 0.01. Even with a more stringent level ($p < 0.001$) some judgement is needed about the social significance of a finding.

Typically tables comparing responses on two variables are presented with actual numbers of respondents in each of the table cells. Here again, the large numbers involved did not make interpretation as easy as it could be. Instead the relevant percentages in the critical categories are recorded. This simplifies the comparison of levels of incidence of behaviour or attitude between the categories of pupil. The results of chi-square tests are not reported as they are almost invariably highly significant. Additional detail, such as the numbers in tables categories, are only given when they help interpretation, or feature directly in the discussion of findings.

Problems with categorisation

Findings are often analysed in terms of sex, age, socio-economic group and ethnicity. Obviously these last two categories are problematic. Socio-economic groupings here are labelled A, B, C_1, C_2, D/E and unclassified in accordance with the Registrar General's classification, which is based on the occupation of head of household. Children themselves designated the occupation of the adults they live with and clearly those designations are open to interpretation in terms of the categories. The normal caveats which would apply to any categorisation of people into socio-economic groups, need to be applied even more carefully in this case.

When considering the children's ethnicity, it is difficult to arrive at clear information and definitions. Children's self-report on this necessarily openly phrased question means that the data may be unreliable, in an area of investigation which is anyway open to debate and discussion. In fact 4.5 per cent of the sample did not provide information on ethnicity. The categories we worked with (question 22) were agreed with the Racial Equality Council. The range of minority groups we ended up with was so large, and the numbers within each group were so small, that for the purposes of the analysis we identified two broad categories: those who identified themselves as 'white', and those who identified themselves as members of other groups. We are aware of the highly problematic nature of this categorisation, but working with the numbers of returns we have, it seemed the clearest way to proceed. The importance of considering ethnicity in relation to children's book choices has led us to maintain this less than satisfactory categorisation.

Categories and coding

Coding of the book list

The book list identifies the school, the individual questionnaire, the book title and the author as given by the child. It also ascribes a number to each book.

The list is sorted alphabetically in various ways to pull together all of the mentions of an individual title.

Titles mentioned more than ten times are considered as a particular group.

The list is coded according to **reader type** and **book type**.

Reader-type categories

1 Child fiction reader
2 Adult fiction reader
3 Non-fiction reader
4 Hybrid reader
5 Unclassifiable, including non-readers

Book-type categories

00 Horror, ghost
01 Romance, relationships and growing up
02 Science fiction and fantasy
03 Sports related
04 Animal related
05 War, spy related
06 Crime and detective
07 Comic books, jokes, annuals, humour
08 Poetry

09 School
10 Adventure
11 Other non-fiction
12 Other fiction intended for children/teenagers
13 Unclassifiable/unidentifiable

Category descriptors

00 Horror, ghost

Fiction in which the narrative is primarily centred around themes of 'horror' or the supernatural.

01 Romance, relationships and growing up

Love stories, including 'adult' and 'teenage' romance. Stories predominantly concerned with adolescent development in terms of family, peer and sexual relationships.

02 Science fiction and fantasy

Stories concerned with future worlds with an emphasis on the scientific and technological. Fantasies, including utopian and distopian worlds, and those which cross historical and time boundaries, sometimes peopled by fantastical characters and creatures.

03 Sports related

Fiction in which the narrative is primarily centred around sporting events and characters (excluding horse-related sports). Also non-fiction related to sports.

04 Animal related

Fiction in which the protagonist is an animal, or in which the prime relationship is between a human and an animal. Also non-fiction related to animals.

05 War, spy related

Fiction in which the setting of the narrative in wartime is central to the story. Stories about spies and spying. Also non-fiction concerned with the military, espionage, or armaments.

06 Crime and detective

Fiction in which the plot centres around crime and its detection. Also non-fiction about crime, the police, and detection methods.

07 Comic books, jokes, annuals, humour

Fiction and non-fiction which uses a comic-strip format. Joke books, children's and teenagers' 'annuals', including music- and TV-related publications. Also books in which comedy and the use of humour are prime features.

08 Poetry

Anthologies of child and adult poems. Collections by a single poet and anthologies which may include both poetry and extracted prose.

09 School

Fiction in which the narrative depends on the school as a setting.

10 Adventure*

Fiction in which action is the prime feature. Picaresque and quest novels. Also accounts of real human adventures.

11 Other non-fiction

Non-fiction other than that contained in other categories.

12 Other fiction intended for children/teenagers

Fiction intended for young people which is not contained in other categories.

13 Unclassifiable/unidentifiable

Titles which can't be placed in any of the other categories because of inadequate information.

---

* Where books clearly fall within two categories, for example school adventure stories, 'adventure' will be considered the subordinate category.

W. H. SMITH *CHILDREN'S READING CHOICES* PROJECT

Questionnaire categories

The questionnaire analysis requires that responses to certain items be placed in devised categories. The following categories have been devised on the basis of responses to the pilot survey:

Item 8: Now write anything you would like to say about the books in this space.

Code responses in terms of judgemental comments:

1 Positive comment, e.g., good, excellent, exciting, relevant, enjoyable, interesting
2 Neutral comment, e.g., 'o.k.', 'alright', quite good
3 Negative comment, e.g., boring, uninteresting, hard to understand, difficult
4 Funny, amusing, etc.

And comments on aspects of the book:

5 Refers to author or series
6 Refers to topic area
7 Refers to film or TV adaption
8 Refers to the way the book is written – the style, or characters etc.
9 Refers to pictures/art work
10 Other

Item 11b: What first gave you the idea to read this author or series of books?

Code responses in the following categories:

1 A parent's encouragement/recommendation
2 A sibling's encouragement/recommendation
3 A friend's encouragement/recommendation
4 Refers to media influence (film or TV connection or audio cassette tape acquisition)
5 Refers to front cover
6 Refers to 'blurb' on book cover
7 School library/teacher influence
8 Refers to public library
9 Refers to advertisement/promotion (other than 5)
10 Other

Item 18(a): Name of Shop?

The pilot survey suggested the initial coding list should include:

Local newsagents
W. H. Smith
Tesco
Sainsbury's
Morrisons
Presto
Finlays
John Menzies
Library sale
Car boot sale
The Post Office
Mail order
Dillons
Waterstones
Computer/adventure games shop
Station/airport/holiday shops
Local bookshop
The village shop
Non-identifiable

This list was added to as the responses from the main survey were coded.

Item 25: I think that reading is . . .

Code responses in terms of judgemental comments:

1   Positive responses, e.g., very good, brilliant, excellent, fun
2   Neutral responses, e.g., 'alright', 'o.k.'
3   Negative responses, e.g., boring, dull

And comments in the following categories:

4   Educational, instructive, 'helps with other work', etc.
5   Good pastime, relaxing, etc.
6   Compared unfavourably to television
7   Other

The interview schedule

Introduction

Swap first names.

I've come from Nottingham University where we've been doing a survey to find out about what young people read. We've got 8,000 replies and now we want to find out a bit more information by talking to some people in schools. We won't be using your name in anything we write and we won't be telling your school what you say. We'd really appreciate it if you could tell us honestly what your opinions are. We won't take longer than half an hour of your time, and we'd like to tape-record the interview so that we can check that we've got all the points that you make. Is that OK?

Questions

1   I want to start by asking you about whether you read any magazines or comics?
    - If No: Why is it that you don't read them?
               Is there anything that you don't like about them?
    - If Yes, and it is the favourite for the child's particular age and sex group: move on to question 2.
    - If Yes, and not the favourite for that age and sex group:

      Have you got a favourite magazine or comic?
      (*bring out a copy of the magazine/comic if available*)

      Why do you like it?

      Which bits do you like best?

2   *Bring out copies of the most popular periodicals for that age (boys' and girls').*
    - We found in our survey that these are the most popular magazines for people your age. (*First consider the one for the same sex as the child.*)

What do you think of this one?

Which bits would you like reading best?

Are there parts you wouldn't read?

- *(Repeat for the other magazine.)*

What do you think of this one?

Which bits would you like reading best?

Are there parts you wouldn't read?

3   Do you ever read magazines or comics more than once?

Which parts do you go back to?

Why?

4   Where do you read magazines?

Prompts – bedroom/classroom/bathroom/with friends

5   When do you read magazines and comics?

Prompts – times of the day/holidays/when ill/weekends/when with friends/in school/on journeys

6   Do you read many books?

- If No: Why not?
- If Yes: Why do you read books?

Prompts – enjoyment/interest/school/friends

7   What would make you choose a particular book?

Prompts – cover, blurb/recommendation(s) (who from?)/TV, film/seen in shop/book clubs, special events/reading about books in magazines, newspapers

8   Have you got a favourite author or series of books?

- If No: Did you use to have
 What was it?
 Why did you like it?
 (Prompts as previous question)

- If Yes: Why do you like that particular writer/series?
 (Prompts as previous question)
 Did you use to have a different favourite author or series
 Who/what was it?
 Why did you change?

9 Is there one book that you really like?

- If No: Have you ever had a favourite book?
           Why did you like it?

Prompts – characters/your feelings/storyline/issues/friendship group discussions

- If Yes: Why do you like it?

Prompts – characters/your feelings/storyline/issues/friendship group discussions

10 Do you like non-fiction books
Prompts – books that aren't stories, information/activity books

- If No: Why not?
- If Yes: Why? What do you like about them?

11 Where exactly do you read books?
Prompts – bedroom/classroom/bathroom/with friends

12 When do you read mostly?
Prompts – times of the day/holidays/when ill/weekends/when with friends/in school/on journeys

13 Do you buy books?

- If No: Why not?
- If Yes: Is it easy to find and choose books in shops?
           If you were the manager of a shop like W. H. Smith, what would you do to help children choose books?

14 We're also trying to find out why people read books that are recommended to them by their friends. Have you got any ideas about that?

- What about books that are recommended by their family? Any ideas about that?

15 We've talked about what makes a book good to read. What do you think makes a person good at reading?
Prompts – amount/book type/speed/level of difficulty

16 We've found out that girls read more than boys. Why do you think that is?

17 Something else we've found out is that boys use computers more than girls. Why do you think that is?

- Do you think that using computers has any effect on your reading?

Prompts – time on computers is time not reading/computers encourage reading certain books or magazines

18 What about television and films – do they make any difference to your reading?

Prompts – time watching TV and films is time not reading/TV and films encourage reading certain books or magazines/programmes about books

19 Conclusion:

OK, thanks. Is there anything you think the people at the university ought to know that's important about young people's book reading or magazine reading?

Thanks very much indeed for your help with this research.

Index